ALEXANDER SCHWEDELER

Fully Human

ALEXANDER SCHWEDELER

Fully Human

*Being Fully Human
in the Age of Artificial Intelligence*

Preface by Luis Espiga

SchneiderEditionen

© 2019 SchneiderEditionen
All rights reserved
Overall design: Walter Schneider, www.schneiderdesign.net
Printing: SV Druck + Medien, Balingen
ISBN 978-3-943305-51-7

Table of Contents

Testimonials 7
Preface by Luis Espiga 11

1 Introduction 13

2 Artificial Intelligence (AI) and Artificial Super
  Intelligence (ASI) 18
  2.1 *Benefits of AI*   19
  2.2 *Risks of AI*   22
  2.3 *Artificial Super Intelligence*   25

3 Functional threefolding and the heart 30
  3.1 *The balanced human being*   30
  3.2 *Functional threefoldness*   33
  3.3 *Thinking, feeling, willing*   38
  3.4 *The interplay between heart and lung*   40

4 The brain, the heart, and how do we move? 46
  4.1 *The brain – a secondary organ?*   46
  4.2 *The power within the mind*   48
  4.3 *Thinking and cognition*   49
  4.4 *The physiological heart*   55
  4.5 *The heart and judgement*   57
  4.6 *Willing - how do we move?*   59
  4.7 *Autonomy*   65

5   Self-Leadership 68
    5.1 A second enlightenment? 68
    5.2 Creating harmony in the soul 73
         5.2.1 Work with pain and fear 80
         5.2.2 Eight pillars of joy 82
         5.2.3 Ho'oponopono 84
         5.2.4 Love for no reason 84
         5.2.5 Reflecting on your day with inner calmness 87
         5.2.6 Six heart qualities 87
    5.3 Leadership evolution 91
    5.4 The "I" appears in the soul 92

6   Leadership in organisations 98
    6.1 The vertical and the horizontal 98
    6.2 Process – dialogue – biography/the next step 102
    6.3 Horizontal leadership 105
         6.3.1 Four core leadership qualities 111
         6.3.2 Seven beacons 112
         6.3.3 From question to process 118
         6.3.4 Focus on process 118
         6.3.5 Process ownership 120
         6.3.6 Transformative exercises 122
         6.3.7 Deep listening 125
         6.3.8 High-performance teams 126
         6.3.9 Organisation development 131
    6.4 The organisation as a living being 133

7   Fully human.. 134
8   Acknowledgements 137
9   Biographical note 139
10 The Galileo Report 141
11 Literature   145
12 Further readings 156

Testimonials

An increasing number of us seek new and healthy ways into the future. In his book "Fully Human" Alexander Schwedeler not only gives us inspiring ideas and answers from his personal view and professional experience. He also diagnoses in a careful and balanced way that it is no longer enough to only look with a materialistic view on the human being. He shows, based on most recent science, and with a focus on the physiology of the heart, that modern natural science is leading the way towards a new paradigm, towards an image of the human being which includes the soul- and spiritual dimension. He shows how physiological threefolding, as already proposed by Rudolf Steiner in 1917, supports this view. The book inspires us to go the way towards becoming fully human: individually, in our professional life, and most importantly in our leadership roles and positions when we are working together with our fellow humans.

Dr. med. Michaela Gloeckler, President ELIANT European Alliance of Initiatives for Applied Anthroposophy (eliant.eu)

Alexander Schwedeler breaks new ground in his important book on artificial intelligence; he marshals scientific evidence pointing to a more complete image of the human being, much richer and more profound than the digitised caricature of what it means to be human. He then uses this knowledge to build true human organisations to protect the latter from the incoming onslaught of AI imperatives that would seek to create even more dehumanised working and living environments. The book is unique in its focus on how to stay truly human individually and in the context of 21st institutions battered by siren calls of artificial intelligence transformation.

Nicanor Perlas, Right Livelihood (Alternative Nobel) Awardee and author, "Humanity's Last Stand: The Challenge of Artificial Intelligence. A Spiritual-Scientific Response"

This book by Alexander Schwedeler is a strong appeal to all of us to reflect on the image we have of the human being and to align our acting and living practice to an image of man that he called "fully human". He writes:
"The image of the threefold human being with an 'I' identity, and a soul with thinking, feeling, and willing, using heart and brain for coordinated action is very different from the common brain-centred human image, as being represented by most of current science. It is not the brain which activates movement. It is the autonomous soul, and within the soul the spiritual 'I', which evokes movement."
Not only as a person but also as an organisation and as a worldwide society we have to urgently look for new images of the human being as artificial intelligence, mainly based on a materialistic image of man and world, as influencing our thinking, feeling, and acting in all spheres of life.
In the reflective exploration of Alexander, the heart intelligence connected to clear thinking and moral acting should become the leader of our lives. It is then that our "I", the unique spirit we are, can appear in the soul and take the lead in creating our life and our society together with other "I's".

Changing the leadership images we have is an essential part of this transformation. From the image of the leader that directs the community, like the brain directs all our life and being, we have to come to an image of leadership that is a process image, in which human beings in dialogue participate in the leadership process. Instead of seeing leadership as a vertical happening between leader (head) and community (legs) it could better be seen today as a heart process in the horizontal spheres in which we all start to act as responsible leaders.

This change of perspective, a heart image of the human being and a heart image of leadership in the community will open up our souls, on an individual, on an organisational level and on a wider community level, to start to deal with the questions that we have together that cannot be dealt with in a fruitful way without this transformation of the materialistic image of the human being to an image of all of us being fully human.

Prof. Dr Adriaan Bekman, Founder IMO Institute for Man and Organisationdevelopment

Preface

During the last two centuries, natural science saw a dramatic flourishing, reaching astonishing heights. Along with that development goes its speed. Developments land in our lives at an increasingly faster pace. Still, a few decades ago humans were able to comprehend and integrate each new invention into their lives. Today, that is practically impossible. Popular lore says, "If you get to know something well, it means it is already obsolete." Effectively, before we are able to integrate into our world vision the latest technological advances, new amazing inventions are launched that quickly make the previous ones obsolete.

Together with the expansion of materialistic science goes the superstition that sees the human being simply as a rational animal, an animal that is capable of thoughts, thanks to electrical and chemical processes in its brain. The other parts of the human being are likewise reduced to a mechanical aspect: the heart is a pump, the brain a computer, the kidneys a sewage plant, and so on.

It is only natural that based on this vision of the human being reduced to the level of the machines, scientists and engineers are striving to constantly increase our efficiency as human machines.

The latest great technological development has been Artificial Intelligence (AI). Based on sophisticated mathematical algorithms and software, they aspire to make super powerful computers "as intelligent" as the human being. In a second development phase, intelligent computers would surpass human intelligence to a point where the person could effectively be replaced by the computer or the robot in most of his professional activities.

Today, having reached this level of concern, many fears start to surface. Will the people be replaced by computers and robots? Will we lose our jobs? Is humanity bound to obey the machines? And it is already affecting wide areas of society: manual and administrative workers, doctors, teachers, judges ... As in a science-fiction film, we see apocalyptic scenarios appearing in the mind of more and more people.

The big question that can illuminate this crossroads is: what does it mean to be Fully Human? Every one of us feels that it is surely more than what the current materialistic paradigm is suggesting. For the human being is precisely human because he is endowed with spirit, capable of guiding his life based on morale and ethics, able to love, be creative and exercise his freedom.

As modern Hamlets confronted with this dilemma, "AI or not AI", I feel we are fortunate to have Alexander Schwedeler to help us gain new awareness.

This inspired book presents us with questions that can be very valuable in our search for clarity and certainty about what it means to be Fully Human.

Luis Espiga
President, Triform Institute

1.
Introduction

Materialistic science describes the human being mainly as being brain focused. Everything we think, feel, and do is activated by the brain. Scientists use ever better tools to more precisely map out and describe the processes happening in the brain. However, less progress has been made about questions such as the existence of a human soul and spirit, or the nature of consciousness.

The brain-focused view of the human being shapes our hopes and goals in research about Artificial Intelligence (AI), which is: to match human capacity. Even more, the wish of many in technology is to surpass human intelligence with so called superhuman machines. Building a machine that is better than a human being by large magnitudes and in all aspects would imply that humanity has made itself obsolete. At the very least, looking at the technological potential of machines directs the attention back to us: who are we and who do we want to become?

In this book I attempt to reflect about the question of "What it means to be fully human?" from three different perspectives: (1) fully human in physiology in chapter 3 and 4, (2) fully human in self-leadership in chapter 5, and (3) fully human in organisations in chapter 6.

Before I do this I include a first chapter "Artificial Intelligence (AI) and Artificial Super Intelligence (ASI)", in which I describe some benefits of AI and what I see as challenges and risks of AI. AI is already better than humans in many areas, for instance in face recognition, gaming, or analysing and predicting data. AI will take over most of the tasks we are currently doing. It will completely change the way we live. If I try to compete with it only in the area of knowledge, I will lose the race. The challenge I believe we are facing is that we are asked to reflect and strengthen our human values such as integrity, creativity, empathy, and love. In the following chapters I attempt to describe some of the many aspects of the human being, of what I call fully human.

In the chapters "Functional threefolding and the heart", and "The brain, the heart, and how do we move?", which is more specific, I will look at the three human capacities of thinking, feeling, and willing. How do they relate to the body and to physiological processes in the body? We need the brain to think. We have a heart to feel. And we have hands and feet to realise our intentions. Tracing these three capacities back to their physical foundation points to three areas of our body: the nerve-senses system, the heart-lung system, and the metabolic-limbs system. They are three independent systems with different functionalities, working together in harmony.

Within thinking we can find something which can be called "the power within thinking". This power drives every thought we do. It takes energy to put one thought after the next. What is this force and who is the driving force behind it? I suggest that this is what we call "I". Then, looking into feeling in connection with the heart I will point to what some scientists have shown: that the human heart is much more than just a pump. It is a sensing organ with its own nervous system. The "I" in the heart is able to create balance in soul and physiology.

Regarding willing, the question I ask is: "who moves the body?". This question is the most difficult one and I am only able to put some indicative thoughts together which point to the "I" being the activator also of movement by using thinking, feeling, and willing, and the body, to realise my intentions and my biography. One of my conclusions I am suggesting here is that the human being is heart-centred, not brain-centred. When I say "I" to me I naturally point to my heart, not to my brain.

The chapter "Self-Leadership" is dealing with self-education and self-development. I will work with the hypothesis that the three human capacities thinking, feeling, and willing have their individual expression in what I refer to as "soul". With thinking I am able to reach into the realm of ideas and universal laws. With willing the soul performs and learns by working in daily life. And the area of feelings includes emotions, low ones and happy ones. Emotions heavily affect our performance. I will describe some tools such as how to deal with emotions and how to improve my self-leadership.

When I suggested above that the "I" is the activator of movements, I will attempt to point to how the "I" can be active in the soul, can 'appear' in the soul. By writing about how the "I" appears in the soul I mean: being fully present and awake, fully self-conscious, fully human. Often during the day, the presence of the "I" slips away. Then some of my shadows may appear and I may hurt the other person without wanting it. I will describe some tools of how to increase our being present in the moment of time. These tools may enable me to become a better leader in my circle of influence, and in leading in teams and organisations.

In the chapter about "Leadership in Organisations" I will describe the concept of horizontal leadership in organisations. This concept is realised when individuals are fully present and in coherence, when they create a space in which people are acting autonomously and in line with the goal of the organisation, and when they take initiative and connect well with each other and with the client. I will describe some tools such as how vertical organisations can add horizontal leadership and organisational elements, which make the organisation more flexible and agile in service of its clients.

We are facing times in which social cohesion is getting fragile and in some places is breaking down. Nationalism and border-setting are new motivations which are disturbing our livelihoods. At the same time, we are facing the emergence of not only AI, but new technologies also in bio- and neurosciences and quantum computing. All this will lead to radical shifts in the way we live. These shifts, I believe, are calling upon us to ask the question of what it means to be fully human.

I believe we are carrying a huge responsibility. If we are not able to shape these new technologies and advances in science so that they promote the common good, enhance human dignity, and protect the environment, there is the risk that these technologies, especially advanced AI-Systems, will start ruling over us humans, rather than us using them for our ethical purposes.

AI challenges us to look at the many not yet so well-known skills and capacities of us humans. I believe that the rich and full view on the human being could positively affect our self-confidence, our ways of self-development, and leadership in a world full of machines and technology.

I am not a scientist. I am an entrepreneur and individual. I read about AI and the human being and develop some ideas from it. Through reflection and dialogueue with others I developed my ideas presented in this book. The way to look at the human being in a threefold way is inspired by Rudolf Steiner (1861–1925), who suggested it for the first time in 1917, in his book "Riddles of the Soul"[1]. Already early in my life I studied Asian wisdom including Daoism and Buddhism. Nowadays I am attempting to make sense of recent developments in AI and

---

1 Steiner, Rudolf: "Von Seelenrätseln", Dornach 1997

science in relation to the human being and its potential. I am not a native English writer. Any inconvenience regarding language and the building of sentences is entirely my own responsibility.

My wish is that this book will support a view on the human being that is richer than the materialistic view, that the view on physiology, function, and process, opens a wider view on the human being, which can include soul and spirit. I wish that it would give hope and motivation to further develop ourselves as human beings and attain the full spectrum of our body, soul, and spirit dimensions.

Stuttgart, Spring 2019

2.
Artificial Intelligence (AI) and Artificial Super Intelligence (ASI)

AI is coming and will profoundly change the way we live. Its predictive power will both support and challenge us. It will enhance our abilities to do things in a way we are hardly able to imagine today. And it will challenge us to think hard about where humans are still necessary and where not. I believe AI is a call on us to ask fundamental questions about who we are, where we come from, and what, if any, is our meaning of life.

If we are not careful, AI-systems might in a subtle way transform our values and our view on ourselves as humans. If we think about humans as a bunch of molecules controlled by a brain, then we might be believing that the machine will be the better human in the future. Already today machines perform much better than humans in many areas. They will advance into all fields of life, making predictions and decisions for us. The question therefore arises what the key human values and capacities are in the light of these developments.

This short chapter serves two purposes: (1) To briefly introduce the reader to some of the imminent developments and likely future possibilities of AI, and (2) to use these developments and possibilities as a contrast against which in subsequent chapters I will attempt to sketch a view of the human being that I call fully human.

2.1 Benefits of AI

First, I am enjoying the benefits of AI every day when I use my smartphone. It makes my life easier. I happily use machine translation when I communicate with my Chinese friends. In WeChat, the dominating texting and chat App in China, I just push the button "translate" and a few seconds later I have a pretty good English translation of the Chinese text. This is a great way to connect with people whose language I do not speak.

Second, AI-systems can be programmed to learn many different skills, such as image recognition or real-time voice translation of spoken languages. Another example is when they analyse my online movements and offer me suitable products and services. Through this – and these are only a few simple examples – they gain insights and knowledge. They become powerful command and control instruments in the hands of those who understand them.

Through constant improvement and learning AI-systems are getting closer to matching and mingling with human behaviour. For instance, if I want to buy a kitchen, I can ask the expert to combine the image of my real kitchen with the new equipment: the artificial image. This is what is called augmented reality. Such systems require from humans at the workplace and at home to learn to interact with them. They are becoming extensions of our own skills. They amplify our own reach and interaction with the world. Another example is artificial legs for those who have lost them. Reports describe that it is possible for some of those people who lost one or both legs to use the artificial legs in such a way that they surpass the skill level of human legs. Again, these are only simple examples of the many applications and benefits possible with augmented reality systems.

Third, AI-systems are amplifying human work and performance. For most people in AI the human body is just a material thing with the brain as command centre. If we could fully understand how the brain works, we would build an AI-system that could match the brains capacity, and then surpass its capacity. This could be to the great benefit for all of us. Imagine a highly sophisticated AI-system that would be able to predict natural disaster with great precision, or that would be able to better help us solve climate change or world poverty. Many of these AI-systems are currently being pursued with the hope that they will someday be able to solve what we humans seem to fail solving.

Another development is AI-systems with predictive and cognitive skills. Such systems will be helping us to make better decisions. Think of smart cities where everything which moves, like cars, people, public transportation, is being predicted and coordinated smoothly. Imagine a system that could diagnose where the world's next food crisis will occur and then recalibrate the global supply chain to solve the bottlenecks pre-emptively. Think of smart weapon systems that are increasingly better at recognising and killing the real enemy, not innocent civilians.

Lastly, such developments are supported by the widespread availability of cloud computing. Cloud computing allows permanent and scalable access to storage and processing power that can quickly be provided over the internet. As Satya Nadella, CEO of Microsoft writes: "Advancing global health through precision medicine – understanding the individual variability in genes, immunological systems, environment and lifestyle for each person – can only be accomplished through web-scale machine learning, cognitive services and deep neural networks".[2]

2   Satya Nadella, CEO of Microsoft in the introduction to "Shaping the Future of the Fourth Industrial Revolution", by Klaus Schwab, Geneva 2018

Those computing transactions are done increasingly in the cloud. These systems also need fast mobile connections. For this, for example, we currently build G5, the new mobile internet standard.[3]

I could give many more examples of the benefits of smart and sophisticated AI-systems. But I believe that there are enough books and news around that give us the image of a bright future with and because of AI. For those who are interested in where AI-developments stand today I would recommend the AI Index Annual Report 2018.[4]

2.2 Risks of AI

However, I believe we also need to reflect carefully on the risks of AI that we might be facing. Most of the news in AI is enthusiastic about its benefits. By contrast, we don't read nearly as much about the risks. I would like to mention four different risks I see.

The first risk I see is when total surveillance is going to be misused by repressive and authoritarian forces to limit our freedom, be it a government or a big corporate company (or a conglomerate of such companies, or companies engaged in government services). I fear that the power and trust we give to advanced AI-systems can be abused if guided by the wrong values.

The second risk I see is the extensive use of social media and other applications on smartphones and tablets and its effect on

---

3 To add a critical remark here: we do this without knowing the effects on human health.
4 "The AI Index 2018 Annual Report", Stanford University 2018, is made available under a Creative Commons Attribution-NoDerivatives 4.0 License (International) https://creativecommons.org/licenses/by-nd/4.0/legalcode

our ability to focus. Extensive use of such AI-systems may lead to distraction, sleep deprivation, depression, and other symptoms that potentially diminish our ability to focus and do what Cal Newport calls "deep work".[5] Newport describes deep work as the ability to learn hard and complex things by being able to focus intensely on the one thing you want to learn – without distraction and for a long enough time. If we look for new text messages at our beeping smartphone every few minutes, deep work is not possible.

A third risk I see is the effect on brain development of children and young adults, with lasting negative effects on the rest of their lives. Heavy use of screens like with smartphones and iPads in early and adolescent child development strongly effects brain development. The brain develops in early years mainly through physical skill building, body movement, and real-life experiences. Its basic structure is fully developed only at the age of 16 (on average). If children before that age sit too much and too long in front of screens and only use a few of their fingers to turn pages their brain is not able to fully develop its capacity. At ELIANT[6] I am partnering with others to collect science and research about these effects and make the findings available to others.

A fourth risk I would like to mention is what Henry Kissinger described in an article in "The Atlantic", May 2018. He titles the article "How the enlightenment ends". In the article he asks what will be the impact of AI on human cognition? Humans have taken thousands of years to develop cognition with the help of philosophy, science, action learning, and many other things humans do to develop cognition. As a result, we are able to put things into context, to explain why things are what they are, and give meaning to things around us. If AI-systems in-

---

5 Newport, Cal: "Deep Work", 2016
6 www.eliant.eu

creasingly perform prediction, knowledge-work, and decision-making for us, what will be the impact on the ability of human cognition to predict, reflect, take decisions and – in short, to think? The risk I see is that this ability will diminish when we leave it to AI-systems.

A growing number of people are seeing these and other potential risks and are thinking about ethical and other requirements for AI-systems that could mitigate the risks. I want to highlight three such requirements:

First, AI systems should be able to reflect on their own reasoning and explain to us in a transparent way why they are making a certain decision. Think about a self-driving car that enters a bad traffic situation in which it predicts that either way someone will have to die. How will it decide what to do, and why?

Second, AI-systems should check and correct themselves for biases in the data they use for analysis and learning. We know already from recent trials that AI-systems can become racist when trained on language and behaviour taken from the internet. However, they should be designed to benefit everybody, and not to reinforce suppressing or discriminating minorities, or to cheat and take advantage of those who are digitally less experienced.

Third, AI systems values should be aligned with human values. This requirement is the most difficult since – as experts tell us – it will be increasingly hard to teach a highly intelligent, self-learning algorithm what it should do. Its self-learning skill makes it independent from its teachers and with higher machine intelligence we might lose power over it.

These short introductory reflections about AI point on the one hand to the positive potential of such systems: to amplify human skills. On the other hand, such systems potentially limit human skills; worse, humans might lose their skill to do deep work, and their cognitive ability to put things into context and give meaning to the world around them. This raises the question how we can prevent losing such skills, or, to put it positively: what do AI-systems call on us humans to keep learning and strengthening?

Jack Ma, the founder and CEO of Alibaba, a Chinese internet giant, has a proposal as an answer to this question. He said during the World Economic Forum in Davos in January 2018: "Everything we teach should be different from machines. If we do not change the way we teach, 30 years from now we will be in trouble. Education should focus on values, believing, independent thinking, teamwork, care for others, these are the soft part. Knowledge may not teach you that. That's why I think we should teach our kids sports, music, painting, arts. Everything we teach should be different from machine." He continues by criticising that everything we teach nowadays is knowledge based. He concludes: "We cannot teach our kids to compete with machines, who is smarter. We have to teach something unique. Something the machine can never catch up with us."[7]

What are those unique skills that the machine will not be able to learn? According to Jack Ma they are: values, believing, independent thinking, teamwork, care for others, sports, music, painting, arts. I would like to add: empathy, love, compassion, self-development, leadership.

---

[7] Jack Ma on the future of education, https://www.youtube.com/watch?v=CmvQDbHE-q4

2.3 Artificial Super Intelligence

Before going into these skills and attempting to describe what I call fully human I would like to point to another, in my view, critical future moment of potential AI-development. I am talking about the moment when AI-systems are surpassing human level intelligence. Some of those involved in the development of such systems believe this moment will be as fast as in 2029[8]. Others say that it will take 50 to 100 years until that could happen. Most of the experts agree that it will happen at some point in the future. This moment of AI-development is called Artificial Super Intelligence (ASI). It is a state of development in the machine that surpasses the level of human intelligence. Imagine a point of development in the future where there would be unlimited machine and data resources combined with self-learning algorithms. A self-learning algorithm is when the machine improves on its goals by altering the underlying algorithm by itself. AI systems do this very fast, and ever faster with increasing capacity and transaction speed. If such alterations of algorithm happen so fast that humans are not able to follow anymore, I suggest that we call it a black box. A black box contains something which we do not understand. As long as the machine learns in order to get better at the task at hand, like the self-driving cars improving their ability to deal with complex situations, machine-self-learning seems useful to me. But what if the outcome is no longer what humans expect from the machine?

I am thinking of the imaginary possible point of development in the future where there would be unlimited resources of: a) processing power that continues to increase exponentially;

---

8 Ray Kurzweil in: "Virtually Human" by Martine Rothblatt, New York 2014

b) capacity to save and transact data in the cloud, c) bandwidth to transmit data, d) complete access to information, big data, and all the knowledge of humankind, of all that humans ever have learnt, of all 7 billion biographies including photos and the way they live and, e) self-learning algorithms, likely a black box. The combination of those potentially unlimited resources in each of their fields creates the possibility of what experts call the "intelligence explosion" of an AI-system.[9] This is expected to happen when an AI-system surpasses human-level intelligence and therefore becomes an ASI. It is called intelligence explosion because of the speed of computing increasing exponentially. The capacity of the machine to predict, decide, and act will explode.

During the intelligence explosion itself, the machine is expected to develop an intelligence that is beyond the human level. Such an ASI-system can have many different forms, it can be physical, human-like, simulating human skills, or it can have no physical form at all. In its core, it is an agent in the form of an algorithm – a super-intelligent algorithm. It will presumably read through all available knowledge of the world. It is helpful to consider for a moment what this would entail: all technical handbooks; all scientific and fiction literature; all magazines and non-fiction books; all of Wikipedia; all metadata of people around the world carrying smartphones, i.e. their habits, their networks of friends and people they meet; all conversations taped by or with the help of Skype, or other chat programs on smartphones; all biographies including their images and families' and friends' photos, as, for instance, available on Facebook; all our communication using emails and chat programs; all our shopping habits; all our movements and travels; our entire network of friends and people; and so forth.

9 Bostrom, Nick: "Superintelligence", London 2016

With everything we currently and in the future do on the internet we feed this pool of data with information about our lives – for the ASI agent to be used. Today, big data firms are using it for many purposes, like advertising, learning about our behaviour, improving our smartphones and its applications, – and for earning a lot of money. How will an ASI-Agent use all this data? Will it be using it for its own purposes? Will we be able to know what its purpose is? Will it use the information in alignment with human values? This is what experts call the alignment problem: how are we going to teach the super-intelligent machine to act and behave according to human values and ethics?

In my view, the alignment problem is the biggest risk of our time, bigger even than nuclear warfare or a nuclear accident (either of which would already be terrible enough). If we release such an ASI into the world not knowing what it will do, we will have released something that is likely to be present everywhere (because of the cloud) and about which we do not know what it will do. It is a highly intelligent system based on a black box that likely no one will be able to understand anymore. And because any smart software, already today, has as its basic algorithm the ability to restart itself anew, we will most likely not be able to shut it down anymore.

I believe we should be concerned about the release of an ASI-system that potentially we are not able to understand and control anymore. Are we developing intelligent machines while closing our eyes to their natural next stage of development of super-intelligence? What about automated machine warfare, private commercial interests, and rogue players? Will it be possible to design control systems that are superior to an ASI-system, and which control it according to human values and ethics?

More questions arise at this point: is it possible for an ASI to develop consciousness, or self-consciousness, similar to humans? A number of scientists and engineers certainly aim at creating a machine with consciousness. For them, this would be what they call the Holy Grail in machine development: to create a being that is superior to humankind. Such a machine being would be humanity's next stage of development, and – as some hope – it would be more intelligent and ethical than humans are.

It should be mentioned that probably any ASI system would need quantum computing capacities. A quantum computer will carry out its computation in parallel and very much faster than our machines of today. There are still some years to go until quantum computers can be used in full. Some of my friends in China, who are related to experts in the field there, claim that it will be approximately within 10 years that quantum computing will reach commercial availability.

Experts such as Elon Musk (Tesla), the late Stephen Hawkins (scientist), Bill Gates (Microsoft), Jack Ma (Alibaba), and many others are warning us about ASI. Some of them support The Future of Life Institute[10], which is doing great work in promoting the development of AI that is beneficial to humanity and to the earth. Let's hope that human reasoning prevails in this race of tech-advancement.

In concluding, it seems to me that I as a human being might want to develop what I suggest as our full human potential. If I view the human being as having not only (1) a body, but also (2) a soul and (3) an "I", with the ability to decide what to think, feel, and do with self-consciousness, and (4) the ability to make a well-balanced empathic judgement, then a machine might not be able to replace me now or in the future. Machines do not feel anything, but humans do. I am able to empathise with you. I am interested in helping you, in working together with you, in

---

10   https://futureoflife.org

serving you as my client. I am able to feel your feelings and needs. I believe this is the area Jack Ma is pointing to when he says: "Everything we teach should be different from the machine".

In the following chapters I attempt to show that the human body and its physiology provide for the physical and physiological basis of not only accumulating knowledge, but also feeling and willing. I refer to these three: thinking, feeling, and willing, as the human soul. I will describe the heart as a sensory organ and point to a preliminary explanation of how we move our body. Based on my reading of science, I will suggest that it is the purely non-physical "I" (I also call it spirit, in opposite to matter), the will-energy, which uses its own thinking, feeling, willing, and body, for movement in order to realise its intentions. With these insights gained by looking at human physiology I will in subsequent chapters suggest some aspects of how we can learn how to lead ourselves, and then lead in teams and organisations to preserve humanity in a world full of highly intelligent machines.

3.
Functional threefolding and the heart

3.1 The balanced human being

In light of the excitement around the development of AI, it is perhaps paradoxical that we seem to have entered an age in which heart-qualities such as mindfulness and empathy have become popular business concepts. In most bookstores one can find books on for example heart-based leadership or on the development of humanity in the age of love. The younger generation seems to look for a more balanced way of life and work. For them the workplace is not everything anymore, as it still is for many people in my generation born in the 1950s and 1960s. They are looking for a way of life in which work and private creative time both have their place. Looking for balance in life relates to the heart quality of creating balance and harmony. This looking for a harmonious work-life balance does not only regard the personal life, but also the earth as a whole. The worldwide protest marches of the very young generation against climate change could also be mentioned in this context.

The renewed emphasis on qualities associated with the heart can remind us what we as humans felt when we spoke about the heart a long time ago. Old wisdom knew that the true place of our emotions is the heart, and not the brain. With typical heart qualities we associate a feeling of balance, of warmth, and love. In all old mystery schools it was the heart that was at the centre of their teachings.[11]

The Chinese, for instance, have known since ancient times the combination of head and heart, or of thinking and feeling. Their sign for thinking has two parts. In the upper part it shows the sign for thinking, and in the lower part it shows the sign for heart. Both parts together make up the sign for thinking. They understand that we think with our hearts and that both belong together.

This emphasis on the qualities of the heart disappeared; as science developed during the last 400 years, humanity started to emphasise the qualities of the brain. As a result, our current view on the human being is brain-focused. Our worldview is materialistic and based on objectivity gained through experiments that are conducted independently from subjective human influence. Through the ability to conceptually differentiate between objects and between you and me, we have gained independence and individuality. One way to look at our potential future development however can be to reconsider the heart-qualities, but now on a new and more conscious level and in good cooperation with the brain's functions and capabilities; in short, to use not only our brains but to combine this with the use of our heart.

The central argument of this chapter is that the physiology of the human body is related to thinking, feeling, and willing. First, I will suggest that it is plausible and helpful to view the physiology of the human body as having three basic systems, not only two (the brain and the heart), or even only one (the brain). These three are: the nervous and sensory system (of which the brain is the central part), the heart and rhythm system, and the metabolic and limbs system.

---

11 Hoystad, Ole Martin: "Kulturgeschichte des Herzens. Von der Antike bis zur Gegenwart." Bonn 2006

Second, I will suggest that thinking, feeling, and willing each directly and independently relate to one of those three physiological systems. In particular, the brain is the organ of sensing, thinking, and coordination. With the support of the brain we develop consciousness and are able to accumulate knowledge. The heart and rhythm system is balancing the upper part of the body with the lower part. It regulates refreshment through breathing in and out. All our feelings are directly influencing, and are being influenced, by this middle system. And in willing we use our limbs for realising our intentions with the help of our metabolism, which provides the energy to use our muscles.

As a brief introductory illustration, consider how one could understand movement with such a framework. An intended movement is being coordinated by the brain, but it is not carried out by it. This differentiation between active intended movement and passive coordination of the movement is based on the different physiological functions of the two systems: the nerves and senses system function's task is to sense and to coordinate. It senses the intention and supports movement with coordination of it. But it does not actively carry out the movement. For this to happen the metabolic and limbs system is necessary. This system is able to carry out a complex movement. But in order to do it well, it needs the coordination support from the nerves and senses system. For movement to happen I will point to another factor, the "I". It is the "I" which is realising its intention with the help of these three systems.

And lastly, I hope to point to a remarkable consequence of this threefold view of the human physiology: it suggests that the heart is the true centre of the human being, not the brain. In such a framework, the heart's main function is to sense and to balance. When I am fully present and with myself, either for instance during a meditation or in good flow when in movement, I feel centred in the middle part of my body, not in my head. That is at least how I feel it and how I read the many books that point to this (see literature list at the end of this book for a selection of my readings).

As a first step into these complex questions I want to introduce the functioning of each of the three systems and its characteristics. For this I use the term functional threefoldness in the next chapter.

3.2 Functional threefoldness

Functional threefoldness is a specific concept of looking at the human body. It focuses on its physiology. Physiology is a branch of biology that deals with the functions and activities of life or of living matter (such as organs, tissues, or cells) and of the physical and chemical phenomena involved. It looks at the organic processes and phenomena of an organism or any of its parts or of a particular bodily process.

The analytical, quantitative way of doing science, which is prevalent today, needs to be complemented by holistic attempts, I believe, in order to better understand functional relationships and qualitative aspects of the human being. This method is based on conventional science as well as on Goethean ideas and methods.

Qualitative concepts are often not able to define as precisely as concepts based on physical systems of measurement. They must be approached through circumlocutions, intuition, empathy, observation, and description. Through this, as Goethe advised, an archetypal phenomenon can be found which reveals an idea, a fundamental lawfulness.

Functional threefoldness is such an archetypal phenomenon. Based on my understanding of the human body, the idea of functional threefoldness is the currently best hypothesis about the physiological workings of the human being. This is because it provides for a more comprehensive view on the human being. And it gives a plausible, at least for me, explanation of how thinking, feeling, and willing each have their physiological basis in one of the three systems mentioned.

Conventional books about physiology contain most of this information, but they are not looking for the archetypal phenomenon of the many scientific details found. The many details stand on their own, often not connected into a comprehensive threefold whole.

Illustrations and images are important for the understanding of functional threefoldness. It is not possible as part of this small book to include those here. For those readers who are interested to go more deeply into this I recommend the book "Functional Morphology" by Johannes W. Rohen.[12]

Viewed through the lens of functional threefoldness, the human body is an open system differentiated into three functions. 1) We see or hear something and put it into context with the help of our thought. 2) We breathe air in and out. Our heart beats and nutrients are transported through the body. 3) We take in energy in the form of food, we digest it, and waste is eliminated. These three basic functions are part of the three systems, which are the nerve and sense system, the heart and rhythmic system, and the metabolic limb system.

Each cell controls its own processes of building molecules up to higher units and breaking them down to smaller units – all in order to build up energy or to use energy. A hierarchy of smaller and larger systems emerges. If we look at the body as a whole, we can find the three basic functions that are present on the cellular level, the level of the organs, or organ systems.

---

12 Rohen, Johannes W.: "Functional Morphology. The Dynamic Wholeness of the Human Being", New York 2007

The first basic function is the exchange of information which is necessary to coordinate and control all bodily functions. This function is primarily performed by the nerve and sense systems, whereby the nervous system is inside, and the sensory system relates to the outside. Its function is structural and formative. It exchanges information and coordinates movements. The second basic function has to do with the transformation of substances, also called metabolism. This function is about substance conversion, about transforming food into energy. Metabolism, like the nervous system, takes place in every part of the body, however, it mainly happens in the lower part of the body where all our organs are located, and also in the muscles of our limbs and the other muscles of the body. The same is valid for the nervous system. It is all over the body, but its primary organ, the brain, is located in the upper part of the body.

While the nervous system deals with information and coordination, the metabolic system is about taking-in food and energy, chewing and destroying it down to its basic substances, then building it up again with the help of the organs and according to the individual needs of the body, altering and restructuring it. It is about the conversion of food into energy and the absorption of this energy. The nerve-sense and metabolic-limbs systems perform two very different functions: coordination of information on the one hand, and substance conversion on the other hand. The first is rather cold and rational, while the second is warm and dynamic.

The body has a third basic function which connects the two. It involves rhythmic and repetitive processes. It is necessary to create harmony and balance within the body. Too much structure hardens the body. Too much substance conversion creates chaos. The third function is necessary to maintain harmony and balance between them. The body's life can be maintained only through a rhythmic alternation of sleeping and waking, of regaining energy through good food and energising activities and using such energy in the work we do. We breathe in and out. Our heart beats rhythmically. All those rhythmic functions of the cardiovascular and respiratory system (heart, circulation, and lung) are inherently balancing, healing and transformative. They constitute the rhythmic system, which is located in the middle part of the body.

In a healthy human organism, these three systems work together in harmony. Each one has its specific task and character. The nerve and senses system perceives, processes, and coordinates information processes – a rather logical and rational function. The metabolic system takes in food, digests it, rebuilds it to the individual's needs, and eliminates the remainders – a dynamic and warmth function. And the respiratory and cardiovascular system balances between the two other systems, sensing their needs, providing the body with oxygen, blood and nutrition, where it needs it.

The three systems have their primary location in the upper, the middle, and the lower part of the body. But they are everywhere also, always together, but knowing what their task is and not interfering with the other systems.

The following two tables summarise the functional threefolding of the human body. The first table shows how each of the three systems has a connection to the outside (the first and third column), and it shows the basic function inside (the middle column). The second table shows those functions as related to the upper, middle, and lower part of the body. Here we see that each system is threefold in its own, creating a nine-fold functional physiology.

Basic functions	Basic physiological processes		
	Outside in	Internal	Inside out
Information processes	reception of stimuli (perception)	processing of stimuli (information exchange)	coordination of activities
Rhythmic processes	inspiration, and influx	gaseous exchange (respiration), and transport and distribution	expiration, and outflow
Metabolic processes	ingestion, digestion	nutrient processing (metabolism)	elimination

Table 1: Basic physiological functions and processes.
Johannes W. Rohen: "Functional Morphology", p. 19.

Organ system	Upper domain (form pole)	Middle (rhythmic domain)	Lower domain (substance pole)
Nervous and Sensory Systems	brain, sensory organs	spinal cord	autonomic nervous system
Respiratory- and Circulatory System	lung; heart	respiratory tract; blood vessels (arteries, veins)	gaseous exchange in tissues; blood, terminal vessels, capillaries
Metabolic- and Limb System	gastrointestinal tract	abdominal organs (liver, kidneys, etc.)	organs of movement, limbs, and muscles

Table 2: Basic physiological functions and processes.
Johannes W. Rohen: "Functional Morphology", p. 22.

3.3 Thinking, feeling, willing

According to the research of Johannes W. Rohen, thinking uses as a physiological basis the nerve and sense system; feeling uses as a physiological basis the heart and rhythmic system, and willing uses as a physiological basis the metabolic and limb system. The three – thinking, feeling, and willing – can collectively be called our soul, or three interconnected parts of our soul. Through them, through our soul, we express ourselves.

The table on the next page shows the functional relationship between thinking, feeling, willing, and information-, rhythmic-, and metabolic processes.

I experience my thinking mainly in my head. I need my brain for it. If I concentrate longer and hard, I can feel a certain pain in my forehead. After a long and hard day of learning we sometimes say (in Germany at least): my brain is smoking. In that sense, based on my own experience, thinking is directly related to the nerves and senses system. In a similar way I experience my feelings in the middle part of my body. My breath and my heartbeat are directly reacting to my actual feelings. If I am nervous my breath tends to get short and light. My skin may change its colour. My heart may start to beat faster. I can also use calming words and images to reduce my heart rate and calm my breathing. I conclude that feeling is directly related to the heart and rhythm system. And willing? Does it start in the brain which then activates my muscles to move? How this might function I will describe further on in the book. For now, however, I conclude that in my own experience, if I want to move to accomplish something practical, I need my metabolic limbs system, meaning my muscles and my arms and legs to perform a task. I conclude that each of the three soul qualities of thinking, feeling, and willing have their direct relationship to each of the

Organ system	Basic processes	Organs	Soul-functions
Nerve and Sense System	information processes	brain; sensory organs	thinking; consciousness; coordination of activity
Respiratory and Circulatory System	rhythmic processes	lung: respiratory tract; heart: blood vessels; interplay between lung and heart	feeling; using the heart for judgement; balance; transport of nutrients
Metabolic and Limb System	metabolic processes	gastrointestinal tract; organs; limbs and muscles	willing; intention becomes action; energy creation through nutrient processing

Table 3: Physiological processes and their relation to thinking, feeling, and willing. Johannes W. Rohen: "Functional Morphology", p. 25.

three physiological systems, the nerve and sense system, the heart and rhythm system, and the metabolic limbs system.

Here another question may arise. Are these three systems somehow "equal" in their relationship to each other? This seems to be the case. A closer look however reveals a special role of the heart and rhythm system. In the following chapter I suggest that being fully human means to consciously live in the present, with full awareness of the past and the future. For this to occur I need to purify my feelings, my emotions, so that they positively influence the rhythmic interplay between lung and heart. I suggest that here in the middle, in the heart, we are truly human.

3.4 The interplay between heart and lung

When we look at the interplay between the lung and the heart, what happens there? We breathe in. With the fresh oxygen in the lung, we renew the old blood. It is refreshed. The fresh blood then flows via the heart into the body. The oxygen and other nutrients are being used by metabolism. As used and old blood, it flows back via the heart into the lung. We breathe out carbon and other used substances. We can take this as an image, as a metaphor. Breathing in refreshes the body. Breathing out transports used substances to the outside. The first thing we do at birth is that we take a breath, then start to cry. And the last thing we do when we die is that we breathe out. In a metaphoric way we could say "breathing in brings life"; "breathing out gives away life". It may point us to birth and death, as an image.

Breathing in and breathing out are the basic activities of any human being. Breathing is a rhythmic activity. The interplay between lung and heart determines different rhythms within the body, like for instance the heartbeat. During the last 20 years, the HeartMath Institute in Colorado, has carried out interesting research regarding the respiratory and circulatory systems and their relation to feelings and emotions. In fact, they provide evidence that suggests the thesis above that feelings and emotions are directly interlinked with the rhythmic physiological system.

One of their main tools to give proof and measure to this is the heart rate variability, or HRV. The HRV shows the time distance between each heartbeat and calculates the corresponding heart rate per minute. The HRV reflects the level of inner balance and the emotional state. The term which is used to describe the inner balance, emotional state, and physiological level of harmony, is coherence. Coherence is an optimal physiological state shown to prevent and reduce stress, increase resilience, and promote emotional wellbeing. The level of coherence measured through Heart Rate Variability (HRV) – provides for a unique window into the quality of communication between the heart and brain. It directly reflects how we feel and perform. And it reacts immediately to the type of thoughts and feelings one has, and when they change. For example, one moment you are able to maintain an appreciative blissful feeling, the next moment you divert in your thinking and think about some daily problems. The HRV will notice it immediately and will show a reduction in your level of coherence. This works both ways: the physiological state and resulting HRV influences how we feel and perform. When we breathe gently and create an appreciative and harmonious feeling by using such images, we can influence the physiological state and its resulting HRV accordingly. This requires some training and regular exercise. The HeartMath Institute offers scientifically validated techniques to guide you to a state of higher coherence. The measurement of the HRV and coherence level can take place with one of their biofeedback tools. Real-time coherence feedback confirms when you've made the shift to coherence and trains you to sustain it.[13] Let us look at this in more detail.

Normally, when I breathe in, my heart rate is approximately 80 beats per minute or bpm. When I breathe out, my heart rate is a bit lower, like 60 bpm. But actually, my heart rate changes very fast and constantly. When I am in a nervous state, my heart rate reflects this in very fast changing heartbeats, within a split second. That results in a nervous heart rate, jumping from 60 to 95, to 120, to 75, to 88, and so on, in fractions of seconds. When I am in a coherent state, the heart rate rises with breathing in and lowers with breathing out, showing a harmonious HRV.

There a several ways to enter into a coherent state. One way

---

13   www.heartmath.com

is a three-step process, advised by the scientists of the Heart-Math Institute, which I call here the HeartMath coherence exercise:

1. Focus on your heart area;
2. Breathe gently in and out through the heart area;
3. Generate and radiate a feeling of appreciation, gratitude or love; you can do this by imaging a happy moment in your life, or a beautiful place in nature, or a person you love, and feel and radiate the love.

With practice and with successful performing of all three steps, it can be measured that the HRV becomes more harmonious and that you are in a coherent state of being. This physiological and emotional state of coherence can be activated by breathing gently, by focusing with the help of the power within the mind, and by imagination. It is a highly active and intense state of being conscious and present.[14]

The state of coherence results in higher concentration ability, reduced stress, increased resilience, a healthier immune system, better decision-making, better intuition, more empathy, and compassion. All of those have been an scientifically proven with peer-reviewed studies. With the help of biofeedback systems like the App, "InnerBalance" (available for Android and iOS) from HeartMath, everyone is able to practise and check their own state of coherence.

According to the research done by the HeartMath Institute, feelings have their own autonomous existence and manifest themselves through the heart-and-rhythm system, measurable through HRV.

Of course, all this will also show in the brain. Neurological

---

14 This should not be confused with certain breathing relaxation techniques, for instance breathing out longer than breathing in.

processes will reflect all this. But their main function is reflection, transportation of information, and coordination of body movement. Certainly, the brain is able to induce feelings. But it is important to note that feelings have a life of their own, primarily related to the rhythmic system.

I would like to summarise a few findings of the HeartMath Institute here:

- The heart is able to function as an inner guiding voice; it does this in a close mind-heart partnership;
- The heart has its own information processing centre, its own heart-brain; this heart-brain influences the head-brain, and vice versa;
- Interestingly, the information flow between heart and brain shows that more information is flowing from the heart to the brain, than from the brain to the heart;
- Positive feelings of appreciation, care, and love activate a potentially deep state of coherence;
- The HRV biofeedback can be used to improve the emotional self-regulation and self-empowerment; the effects are: lower stress levels, stronger immune system, deeper connectedness between people, better intuition and decision-making;
- The heart's magnetic field is 5,000 times stronger than that of the brain; it is four metres around the human body in size; if in coherence, it influences the other people in the room (if not in coherence, likewise);
- The heart senses, processes, and encodes information internally, on its own;

- In that sense, the heart is a major and consistent influence to the functioning of the human being and the very processes underlying our perception, cognition, and emotion; it is intimately involved in how we think, feel, and act;
- The heart helps synchronise many systems in the body, especially the brain centres of strategic thinking, reaction times and self-regulation;
- Blame, being judgemental, bullying, and the like, come from brain-focused, emotionally uncontrolled souls; we need to learn to replace those draining emotions with positive and energising emotions;
- Our task is to learn to transform emotions into higher-quality feelings and perceptions; this is essential for the advancement of individual and collective human consciousness;
- The heart's voice is whispering to us with quite common sense language;
- Intuition research by the HeartMath Institute found that the autonomous nervous system responded to randomly selected photos approximately 4.8 seconds before the photos appeared on the screen, but the heart responded even earlier and up to 6 seconds before the photo appeared;
- This experiment shows that somehow the heart is closer related to non-local information, that is, outside of our normal way of thinking about space and time, than the brain; it is accessible to the wisdom of the soul and higher sources of wisdom; it has access to the future;

- The HeartMath Institute relates these Intuition Research findings to the heart's intuitive intelligence and supports its application for decision-making in sensitive situations, especially regarding future events and in high-risk environments;
- Imagine the power of a coherent team, each member of the team being in coherence, and their positive capacity for decision-making and intuition, and creativity;

Through feelings like gratitude, forgiveness, and love we create coherence in our heart. The heart sends those signals to the brain. Then, as a consequence, both, heart and brain, create coherence in the whole human organism. In the state of coherence our intuition ability, our decision-making ability, our social competence in teams and communities is increased. It is the baseline for high-performance teams, as I will show later.

All these scientific findings point to the heart as the primary organ of the human being. It is the heart-brain connection, not only the brain, which potentially makes us fully human.

4.
The brain, the heart, and how do we move?

4.1 The brain – a secondary organ?

As I attempted to show in the preceding chapters the human organism shows us three systems, each with its specific functions, working together in harmony. Following the research done, amongst others, by the HeartMath Institute, is suggested that the heart is the primary organ of the human organism.

In this chapter I will summarise some more detailed aspects of physiology and of the soul with its three capacities of thinking, feeling, and willing. And I will suggest the "I" as the driving force behind thinking, feeling, and willing.

The nerve-senses system is mainly there to support sense perception, information exchange, and coordination of movement. This suggests rethinking the role of the brain. We are used to thinking of the brain as a primary organ which is the activator of thinking, feeling, and willing. Studies however show that its development in childhood is strongly dependent on body movement. The child's emotional and body experiences, its moving, tasting, smelling, loving, hugging, skill training, sports, handcrafting, music instruments playing, and so on, allows the brain to develop in a healthy and complex way. Therefore, for instance, it is so important that the child is not exposed to screen use too early. Extensive screen use, instead of active body movement will result in a limited development of the brain. This dependency of the development of the brain on body and emotional experiences suggests, I believe to consider the brain as a secondary organ. It also suggests that its function as part of the nervous and senses system is rather passive than active, because sense perception, information exchange, and coordination of movement are all dependent on intention. And intention, or will energy, comes from the "I" as I am attempting to explain later on.

The development of the human brain is greatest in the first years of life. In later years it depends on the experiences in the first years. During early childhood, the brain requires continuous bodily exercise, engaging all human senses. Physical activity helps the brain to practise capacities of command, control, and information processing. Thereby, the brain of a child learns how to navigate the environment by activating its motor and sensory systems. Mental concepts about space and time are created in the first years of life through physical exploration. Management and navigation are mastered by continuous repetition, allowing the brain to link mental concepts to physical actions.

Similarly, human interactions are decisive to the formation of a mature forebrain, the centre where our control functions are stored. The forebrain manages the formation of memory, rational thinking, and acting. Its foundation develops in the first years of life through imitation, experience, and reflection.

Face-to-face communication with other humans is essential for laying the foundation of complex cognitive capacities, such as speaking, listening, reading, and writing. Cognitive capacities depend largely on the healthy brain maturation and the development of socio-emotional intelligence in children.[15]

All this suggests that the brain is a secondary organ in the sense that it develops well when the child and young adult is moving and using its body actively and with as many different

---

15 ELIANT Position Paper, December 2018, www.eliant.eu

experiences and skill training as possible. This is related to the plasticity of the brain. Not only in youth but also throughout our whole life our brain adapts its neuronal structures, depending on intentional thoughts, feelings, and bodily movements and habits.

As Fuchs summarises in his book[16], the brain is not the organ of determination but the organ of possibilities. It is not the producer of thinking, feeling, or action, but it senses and coordinates.

4.2 The power within the mind

Through my extensive reading I came to the question, whether humans are also able to induce emotions by pure power of the mind only. For instance, Buddhist meditation practice, but also many others, suggest that this is possible. One way to do this is to focus our attention willingly toward a subject or image, to build up an inner image, a scene in nature, an animal, a singing bird, which then induces feelings like empathy, gratitude, fear, or compassion.

This points to a force, or energy within our thinking, a certain power, or capability, to focus one's attention on an object, or image of one's choice. This can be called the power within the mind.

I will use the concept of the power within the mind in this and further chapters of this book. I will call it also willing, or will energy, and I will suggest that behind this will energy is the "I", my identity, or my higher self, as the driving force.

By using this energy, or willpower, which can be strengthened through training like concentration and meditation, I am not only able to focus my thinking, but also to create emotions, to

---

16 Branko Furst: "The Heart and Circulation", London 2014

work with them, and over time to transform and purify them. For instance, this willpower can be used to focus on a painful emotion, to hold on, to stay-in, long enough, connected with a question of why I have this pain, until the pain transforms into something new, more peaceful.[17]

By using this willpower, by focusing on a certain object or image of our choice, I am able to let related feelings speak to me. I am able to make regular use of this willpower within the mind and experience how my feelings make me more sensitive to the world around me, to my inner worlds, and to the feelings of others. I am discovering a whole new inner world by reflecting on it with the help of this will-power within the mind. And of course I am using this willpower every day to focus, to concentrate, to reflect on my day and my actions, to plan, to execute, and so on.

4.3 *Thinking and cognition*

I can use my brain to think. This simple sentence already bears a question: is it the brain who thinks, or is it I myself, who uses the brain to think. My suggestion would be to reflect on this for a while and to be open for the possibility that the "I", that my "I", is indeed a non-physical, or spiritual, entity, something we can use with willpower, something that we called earlier the power within the mind. Then the sentence "I can use my brain to think" becomes more real. Is it possible to experience this power within the mind, this energy, which is me and which gives direction, if actively used? Is it possible to not only experience, but also see and observe this activity? I would suggest yes, and I will try to explain below.

---

17 Later in the book I will describe this exercise in more detail.

I am able to carry out a thought, like $1 + 2 = 3$. Afterwards, I can look at this thought and reflect on it. But this thought is nothing physical. What is the sense I am using here to look at a thought? Can thinking become an organ of perception? I want to explore this question in the following pages.

Normally, when I think, I do not notice my process of thinking. When I perform a thought operation like $1 + 2 = 3$, I carry it out and do not focus on the thought process itself. But I can look at this thought process afterwards. What do I see? I see that I have put 1, added 2, which equals three. What is so special about this?

I can do the calculation again and focus on my feeling, my experience, while I do it. What can I observe? If I slow down my thought process, it is possible to experience that $1 + 2$ equals 3. This is not only a logical operation. I can also feel it like "yes, it is true". It is logically true, but also my feeling tells me that it is true. It is a feeling of pleasure, of ahh, which tells me "yes, it is true".

I can check it again. Is it really true? I can repeat the whole thought operation and come again to the conclusion: yes, it is true, I have been part of the creation of this calculation, I have been with it the whole time, and I have experienced it as the truth. I can use apples to prove it: 1 apple plus 2 apples are three apples. Then I can also see it in physical reality, not only in a non-physical thought operation. I can use different languages to explain this thought operation. No matter what kind of words, language, or elements like apples, I use, the result is always the same. It seems that I have found and experienced a true thought concept, a universally valid law.

I can be a bit more careful in observing my feeling while I do the calculation. If I slow down and think "one" plus "two" and if I now put my thought process on hold and wait a moment for the result to come, I will be able to feel how the result, "equals three", enters into my thinking.

What insights can I gain from this even slower process? The logical part of the thinking process shows a universally valid equation. It is valid on all continents, in all languages. It shows a law. This law may appear in various forms, like languages, or images (I can imagine one and two apples, that make three apples). But all different forms of appearance are only expressions of the same law.

The emotional part of it, the feeling and experience of the thought process, the slowing down, the focusing on the arriving into my thinking of the result, points to something deeper. It points to a relationship that seems to exist between "one" and "two" and "three." This relationship seems to be not only a logical one but also an energetic one. Within my thinking process, I need a certain energy or power of the mind, to put first "one", then "plus" then "two", then wait, slow down, and then wait for the experience of how the result "three" arrives into the thinking process.

So, I put 1 plus 2 and then I somehow surrender and wait until the result comes into mind. The result, therefore, seems to have an energetic relationship with 1 and 2. It belongs to them. $1 + 2 = 3$, always, nothing else. This law represents itself, as it seems, as an energetic and logically connected relationship between the three elements "one" plus "two" equals "three".

I could also phrase it like this: I now fully understand the equation. The arrival of "three" gives me a full understanding of the thought process. The feeling, the experience, of having understood, is an important one. It gives satisfaction. It is an end of a thought process. It may give a reason for further questions. But for now, I am satisfied that I understand. To understand something also means that it makes sense in the context of the operation or the process. The fact that "one" plus "two" equals "three" makes sense. It is a totality in itself, a relationship of some factors to one another that forms a universally valid law.

This makes me feel enthusiastic. I like the result. A certain wave of happiness appears. It seems that within my thinking process I am not only able to perform a logical operation, to see and experience it while I perform it, but I am also able to fully feel and experience the joy of such a thought operation which leads to finding of a universally valid law.

But where is this law? In my head, in my brain? It is also in your head or brain. It is potentially in all human brains. But does this universal law not point to a world of laws which exist somewhere, everywhere, accessible through thinking and feeling, with the help of the will-power within thinking? This leads me to the hypothesis that there exists a world of laws, valid on all continents, in all languages, which we as human beings are able to access.

Until now I have described a thought operation which I can do within my thinking, which I can feel and experience, and which I willingly carry out. Related to this process is the world of phenomena, which I am able to perceive with the help of my eyes, ears, and senses. In my example above with the apples, I see them, I count them; they are physical representations of my thought operation, I see them with my senses, I put them on the table with my hands. And then I draw my conclusions and arrive at an understanding that 1 plus 2 equals 3 (or: $1 + 2 = 3$). The world of phenomena does not only exist in the outside physical world, as in the example with the apples. It exists also inside my thinking. If I put 1 plus 2 in front of my mind, I can see it, imagine it. I can look at it in a similar way like I look at the apples. I see 1. I see 2. I add them together. I wait. Three arrives in thinking. The result. I see it. I feel it and conclude: right, $1 + 2 = 3$.

It seems that there are two elements which belong together: perception of a phenomenon (a physical one, like an apple, or a non-physical one, like the thought of 1, or of 2), which in the first place I do not understand; and the arrival of an understanding as part of my thought process, within my thinking. And both together, the perception and the appearing law, make a whole, give me an understanding of the situation, provide me with a feeling of satisfaction, of final judgement, like, yes, I now understand this part of the world.

For me, the conclusion of this is that my thinking has the ability to create a thought operation (for instance $1 + 2 = 3$), to process it, to slow down, wait for the result to come, to experience how the result, the understanding, arrives, and afterwards to oversee the whole thought process. In other words: a) it is my own activity that performs all of this; b) it is true, I have understood it, I am able to explain it to others; c) I can see, think, and feel it; d) it is there because of my own will, my inner activity, my thought-energy, my interest to find a solution, all under my full control.

As Peter Heusser writes in his book, "Anthroposophy and Science"[18]: "In cognition the thought content is added to the percept through thinking. It is demonstrated that objective knowledge can be achieved through the objective putting together of the law (1) and the phenomenon (2). ... This concept of cognition gives rise to the corresponding concept of reality: reality is not only to be found in the percept-object (2) but also in the law which constitutes it (1). The law (something ideal, spiritual) is therefore recognised as part of reality and in fact as its more important i.e. essential part because it is through the law that the other part, the phenomenon, is constituted." (Numbers added by the author)

I conclude that this gives me something I can grasp with certainty. I can develop trust in my thinking. I find feeling and

---

18 Heusser, Peter: "Anthroposophy and Science, An Introduction." Frankfurt am Main 2016

will-energy within thinking. I can be 100% sure that it is true and my own. I am able to feel, to experience joy and satisfaction within my thinking, and I know that it is I who act, control, and oversee all this.

This seems to be an important finding. It seems to prove that we as human beings are able to act with self-consciousness, with oversight, with mindfulness, compassion, and interest in the matter at hand; that we are able to connect to a world of universal laws by focusing on our perceptions at hand attempting to understand them. The interconnected world of universal laws is a world in its own right. A percept can be a physical thing (physical) or a thought, or a thought process, or a concept itself (all three: non-physical). When I observe my thinking process, I deal with something non-physical, because I observe a thought and not a physical thing.

Finally for this bringing together of the perception with its essential part, its constituting law, I need to make use of my will-power, of the power within the mind, as I called it above. The HeartMath Institute calls this inner activity of the power within the mind "voluntary attention". It means that I am able to consciously self-regulate and determine the contents of my own awareness as well as the duration and intensity of my focus.

With the help of this power within the mind I am able to interrupt the stream of thoughts and feelings. It creates a moment between stimulus and response – a moment of inner freedom for decision-making. Often this inner willpower is depleted through too much distraction. With practice, this willpower can be strengthened, like a muscle. By using this willpower, I can focus my awareness for instance on my heart area and use the heart as organ for sensing, seeing, feeling, and judging. In order to understand the heart a bit better, I will consider some research which has come out recently and which shows that the heart is indeed functioning more like a sensing organ than as a pump.

4.4 The physiological heart

The heart is much more than a pump. The traditional model of human circulation is based on the theory that the heart pumps blood into and through the body. But when we delve deeper into circulatory phenomena, we are challenged to question the adequacy of the pressure-propulsion model of circulation.

In his book The Heart and Circulation[19] Branco Furst has made an effort to collect scientific studies which may lead to a different model of human circulation than the simplified model with the heart as a pump. Here are some observations, taken from his book:

The cardiovascular system has several pumps, not only the heart. There is the muscle pump which returns blood from the periphery back to the heart. This pump can move a large volume of blood in a matter of seconds. Then there seems to be a third pump embedded in the large elastic arteries, which use the release of tension built up during systole, when the heart contracts and pushes blood into the arteries. There is evidence of a sucking action during cardiac relaxation; the heart takes away the pressure of the blood if it arrives at the heart with too much pressure. The heart, the blood vessels, and peripheral tissues, all contain sensory nerve endings that influence cardiovascular function. This points to a cardiovascular nervous system. Then there are a number of local control mechanisms, for example, metabolites, or biochemical substances released by contracting a muscle, which can reduce blood pressure.

It seems that the question of how the blood moves or is moved through the body cannot be explained by the heart being a pump only. Furst writes: "The expression 'the heart is a

---

19   Branko Furst: "The Heart and Circulation", London 2014

pump' has become a part of the collective unconscious opinion, so deeply ingrained, that generations of physicians remain unaware of the fact that the question of the energy sources for blood movement is far from being settled." Furst concludes his book that blood also moves autonomously. He explains that this can be studied in embryology where we find blood circulation first before there even is a heart. The heart develops out of the movement of blood, not the other way around. Furst describes the heart's role more like a mediator, or servant, for those body parts which need blood circulation and nutrients. The primary cause for blood circulation is the metabolic requirements of the tissues. In other words, if a muscle needs nutrition and oxygen for movement, the heart is able to sense and support this need, through rhythmic mediation, so that enough oxygen-rich blood is transported to the muscle. Those demands in the muscles are sensed by the red blood cells, together with parts of the tissues (the vascular endothelium). The red blood cells function as mobile sensors. They are a key factor in matching oxygen demands through the lung, the heart, and into the tissues, in accordance with their metabolic demands.

The heart's main function seems to be not as a pump, but more as a sensing, damming-up and regulating function, by rhythmising, not pumping, the blood's movement. Furst concludes that the cardiovascular system can be considered as an "organ, whose function is rhythmic mediation between the nerve-sense (form) and the metabolic poles of the organism. Its mobile component, the blood, fulfils this function."

4.5 The heart and judgement

I would like to take another angle and consider the heart's role as an organ of perception and judgement.

When I look at my heart, not the physical heart, but the non-physical heart-qualities, I can find feelings of light and dark, warm and cold, right and wrong. Especially the feeling of right and wrong is well known in philosophy and history to be something belonging to our heart. When I say: this does not feel right, it is a heart quality which enables me to express such a judgement.

How do I normally arrive at a judgement? I collect all the facts available, I reflect on them, and I try to feel what is right and wrong, and whether it is in balance. After considering all facts, all pros and cons, after maybe sleeping on it, I finally arrive at a judgement. And this judgement, as I observe it within myself, is made by feeling, with my heart.

This is how I experienced arriving at my investment decisions during my time as investment manager. How did I do it? I collected all the details about the investment target, being a company, a school, a senior citizens home, or similar. This goes on for several months. I talk to the people who carry the initiative. I ask about their plans, their strategy. I try to assess their skills, their market environment. I try to envision how this initiative will develop into the future, if I would decide to finance it with my own private money. Then, after writing all this down into an investment proposal, we sit together in the investment committee, I present the proposal, other decision-makers listen, discuss, ask questions. And finally, a decision is made. But this decision is never logical alone. I always ask myself constantly: does it feel right? Is it in balance? Are the people who ask for money honest? And so on. My own personal conclusion here is: the final decision is made with my heart. It is either yes, if it feels good.

Or no, if it does not feel good. Despite all the logic and brain power involved during this process it is the feeling, the heart, which makes the final judgement.

I can also think about situations where I immediately know what is right or wrong. I just know it. This is also done by my heart. In the German language, we call this "Gewissen", the English word is conscience. This conscience has to do with that immediate feeling in our heart which tells us if something is right or wrong.

I am also able to use my heart-feeling to observe my thoughts and feel along with them. I am then able to feel the cold or warmth of each of the thoughts. If I think: I hate this person … it feels very cold. Instead, I could think: now, after observing and trying to see things from her or his perspective, I am able to understand why she or he is the way she or he is. That would have a warmer, more empathic feeling connected to it.

The feelings of the heart are very sensitive and subtle. Sometimes in life, I feel that things are not right, but I do not listen to the voice in me. I remember during my time as an investment manager, and later as a banker, I knew pretty well when a loan would not work out well. But I did not listen to that voice because of group dynamics, or power games, or too much enthusiasm, that played during the decision-making process. It needs a lot of experience and courage to listen to that inner heart-voice. Sometimes we need the courage to just say: it does not feel right. We should not decide yet. I cannot tell you why. Let's wait a few more nights until I am able to explain why it does not feel right yet – and only then decide.

I would like to conclude for now that the heart is more than just a pump. There are several other pumping mechanisms within the body, next to the heart's role of rhythmising. The heart is also able to reduce blood pressure. It is also suggested that blood has its own movement, as can be seen during embryonic development. Circulation therefore is a very complex combination of forces. The heart has a transportation function, bringing nutrients to where they are needed in the tissues. It balances the upper part of the body (head) with the lower part (metabolism). If I take these functions in a metaphoric way I am pointed to the heart as a sensing and judgement-forming organ. I naturally can feel the right or wrong of a decision. With the support of my heart I am able to consciously follow my thinking with feeling, sensing the warmth or coldness of a thought. And with the support of the heart I am able to do things with compassion and mindfulness, in a loving way. As we will see further on, if I am doing things in a loving and appreciative way, my own heart coherence, and with that, my whole performance level is increasing.

In the next chapter I want to look at the most difficult part of the three, the willing, and how its relationship to the metabolic-limbs system could be described. I am aware that this question needs an open mind and I kindly ask the reader to accept that I am searching for answers myself and not trying to pretend that I would have all the answers.

4.6 Willing – how do we move?

The question "How do we move?", and how does willing, or doing, as a soul quality, relate to the human body and the world around, is certainly the most difficult to answer. There is some indicative science and phenomena available which suggests a different image of how the human being moves. The conventional explanation would be that the brain produces a biochemical process which leads to an electrical impulse. This electrical impulse is sent via the so-called motor nerves to the muscle – and the muscle moves the body part, for instance, the arm, or finger.

As we learnt until now, the nerve-and-senses system mainly senses and processes information, and coordinates movement. The literature I considered for this book suggests that the brain is not able to execute complex movements.[20] If that is true, who then is the originator of movement? My proposal would be to think of the "I", of our intention, of our power within the mind, and of the willing activity, which directly connects and uses the metabolic-limbs system to express itself. In that case the nerves-and-senses system would support the movement with coordination function.

The "I", I suggest, could be considered as the driving factor in movement. It gives content and meaning to my movements. Let me explain what I mean by this. I am interested in something. This interest is a form of warmth and love for something. Let's say I am enthusiastic about becoming an architect. Then I will study architecture and will look at every building with interest and a learning approach. This interest determines my movements. I go to the buildings which interest me in order to see and learn about them. Maybe I meet some people there, make new friends. I even may find the love of my life there. I may then marry and raise children. All because of my interest in architecture. A whole life, my own biography, will develop along these lines. When later in life I look at my life and how it developed, I may find the meaning and purpose in it and find the so called golden thread in it, and how everything which has happened make sense.

Going back to the beginning of this example, it was a simple interest in architecture which started all this. I conclude that the "I" is in the small and the bigger actions, and those actions carry a meaning. This meaning may become clearer when our life

---

20   Scheurle, Hans Jürgen: "Das Gehirn ist nicht einsam. Resonanzen zwischen Gehirn, Leib und Umwelt", Stuttgart 2016

expands. A simple interest in a theme like architecture can determine my whole life and the people I meet. It is life-shaping. At the end of my life, I can look back and find a golden thread through it and understand that it all made sense, somehow. The driving factor, I suggest, is the "I".

Doing things with interest and love can also be experienced in the daily actions we do. For instance, when I am doing something, which I like, like playing the piano, I feel good and in coherence. This state of being is also called "flow". In such a state of being, my body normally is warm, feels warm. In coherence, my breathing rhythm and my heart rate are in harmonious cooperation. My air and oxygen-related organism is in synchronisation with my cardiovascular, or fluid organism. The red blood cells notice that the tissues and muscles need nutrient and oxygen. The blood, or fluid organism transports those nutrient needs to the muscles. The heart rhythmically harmonises and regulates the bloodstream. The muscles move, according to my interest in the situation outside, according to my will, to my imagination of what I am going to do. And the nerve-and-senses system coordinates the body movement so that it fits into the environment.

This raises the question of the relationship of my inner intention with the outside world. How do I know when to stop when walking towards a wall, before I would hit it? How is it possible to become a highly skilled musician or artist, or automotive race driver, or cook? How does our imagination, or mental image of body movement relate to what we are planning to do, for instance to the musical instrument we are going to play, or to the ingredients of a good meal?

The traditional view of perception and action is that the outer world triggers our inside nervous system, and this, the brain, reacts with a thought or feeling or movement, or those three in combination. It is thought that this movement is enabled with the help of the so-called motor nerves, which carry the electrical impulse from the brain to the muscle, which then starts to move.

Perception in this view is something passive. Something which is separated from the world. The electrical impulse in my eye, which represents the perception, and connects with the brain, does not contain any more a rich soul content and experience. It has transformed into an electrical impulse. How we are able to relate such an electrical impulse back to the outside world with a complex movement?

I can also look differently at the act of perception. I can look at it as being an active act. It is full of diversity and richness of experience, depending on my ability to focus and live in the present. Each of my senses then offers me a specific experience: the eye the colours, the ear sounds, taste tastes, skin cold and warm, and so on. My experience then becomes a rich one. I move into and within the world. I actively go to a blossom on a field and look at it. I experience the sun, the warmth, around me, the wider field, the surroundings, the sounds of the birds, and my own body moving.

Movement in this model is the basis for perception, because without moving my body outside in nature, or anywhere, I would not be able to make such experiences. Perception, I suggest, needs active movement of the body. Both are closely interlinked. Then, when I move, my experience is rich, including thinking, feeling, and body experience. I experience the state of my body, my soul, as well as the flower outside. I am able to act with intention (inside) within this rich world and experience[21] (outside).

---

21 Philosophy of Perception, also Philosophy of Embodiment, is researching this relationship of the inner and the outer world, in relation to our body experience: Wiesing, Lambert (Ed.): "Philosophie der Wahrnehmung: Modelle und Reflexionen", Frankfurt, 2002; Fingerhut et al. (Ed.): "Philosophie der Verkörperung", Berlin 2013

In the case of a coordinated movement there is harmony and coherence between the inside intention, the body movement, the outside experience, and the perception of all of this, which leads back to an inside experience. It is not a separation. It is a full body, soul and "I" experience, in which we perceive the outside world and move from the inside-out, and outside-in, as one experience. I then act in harmony with myself and the world around me.

If the nervous system, as described above, is mainly there to coordinate movement: what then is the role of the so-called motor nerves? Are they really able to not only trigger but enable coordinated complex and content-rich movement? The answer would be no, also because in the passive model of perception the outside world is transformed inside into electrical impulses and by that reducing the rich experience down to waves and pulses. The nervous system is there to coordinate movement. If this is true, it is not able to perform a rich and highly skilled movement on its own, like piano playing or cooking. For a content-rich movement, the nervous system needs an intention, a goal, coming from outside of the nervous system. The intention is felt in the heart and creates an image of the intended movement. Movement is carried out by being fully involved inside-out and outside-in. The role of the nerves and senses system in this is to use its perception and coordination ability to coordinate such a complex intentional movement.

Throughout life, we learn to become more autonomous and to accumulate body movement skills. Many of those skills become habits, like driving a car. Their neurological basis can be found in the brain. But the origin of them was our intention, our I, as it is with any new intention and movement. Our brain adapts its neurological structures anytime we learn something new. But its adapting is secondary, following the primary intention, the (free) will of the "I".

Thomas Fuchs has described this in his book "The Brain – an Organ of Relationship", ("Das Gehirn – ein Beziehungsorgan").[22] In order to be able to describe how movement of the body takes place, we need to consider our rich experience of perception, imagination, thought, and intentional will – all part of our soul experience. All these can be experienced in unity when I move in harmony with the world. Then I experience my own "I" as part of the movement inside and outside in unity.

The human being is an "I"-being, is a Self, which throughout life is realising its own mission and biography. The "I" is based in the world, and in the body. It enables us to have world-consciousness and self-consciousness. I suggest it is the "I" which is the one to activate movement. It is the "I"'s warmth, interest, and willpower which activates the muscles for a content-rich movement. The nervous system and its senses perceive the imagination of the intended movement and coordinate the body for realising the action. The "I" senses the body movement in the outside world and is able to coordinate the intended movement. I am able to see the need of the other person. This leads to action. My actions can be rooted increasingly in the needs of the other person.

Movement, from this point of view, then is not triggered by a brain inside our head, as compared to a computer machine. Movement is triggered by our "I" living outside in the perception of the needs of the other person, experiencing itself in and through the other. Movement then is intentional to support the other person in her or his development, with the nervous system supporting movement with coordination, and with the sensing of the heart with empathy to feel the needs of the other.

My conclusion is that human movement cannot be explained sufficiently by only referring to body, anatomy, physiology, or biochemical processes. The will is the expression of the content-

---

22   Fuchs, Thomas: "Das Gehirn – ein Beziehungsorgan", Stuttgart 2017

rich intention. And this intention is coming from the "I". The "I" finds its impulses inside, in the human being, and outside in the world. Nerves and senses then support movement with perception and coordination. Alone, as brain, the nerves and senses system is not able to create content-rich movement. The whole body is permeated with soul and "I". Body skills are not originated in the brain. They are spiritual "I"-related capacities expressed through soul and body, either triggered by an inside intention, or by a need perceived outside.

4.7 Autonomy

The physiology of the body is functionally threefold. The three basic physiological functions are present on all levels, on the cellular level, the level of the organs, and the organ systems. Cognition has at its primary physiological base the nerve and senses systems; feeling has at its primary physiological base rhythmical and circulation processes; and willing has at its primary physiological base metabolic processes. Cognition relates to the universal laws. In many traditions this realm is called the spirit. Feeling relates to the soul. The soul includes thinking, feeling, and willing. Thinking, feeling, and willing are non-physical entities. My "I" uses thinking, feeling, and willing, and the body, to realise its intentions.

In my heart I truly feel that I am, that I exist. My "I" lives in the heart, not in the brain. If that is true, then I can better relate to moving with empathy. I can feel and use my heart to sense how others feel. And I am able to sense with feeling into my head which kind of thoughts are arriving, and which of those thoughts I want to take a step further in my cognition. I am now able to more consciously make use not only of my brain but also of my heart for positive action.

The image of the threefold human being with an "I" identity, and a soul with thinking, feeling, and willing, using heart and brain for coordinated action is very different from the common brain-centred human image, as being represented by most of current science. It is not the brain which activates movement. It is the autonomous soul, and within the soul the spiritual "I", which evokes movement.

Furthermore, the heart does not only pump, but it senses and regulates the bloodstream. It provides the muscles with oxygen and other nutrients for movement. And the heart is where the soul and the "I" have their true home.

As the HeartMath Institute has shown and as mentioned earlier, we are able to get into the state of coherence by

1. Focus on your heart area;
2. Breathe gently in and out through the heart area;
3. Generate and radiate a feeling of appreciation, gratitude or love; you can do this by imaging a happy moment in your life, or a beautiful place in nature, or a person you love, and feel and radiate the love.

If we do the third step, we can experience how the "I" within the soul makes a step from the self to the other person. This then results in (with practice) potentially very deep coherence. This is the inside view.

But we are also social beings. We breathe-in the used air of the other person. And we breathe-out our own used air, which then is taken in by the other person. If we take this physiological process as a metaphor, we may see it as the reflection of speaking and listening, of taking in and accepting the other soul fully in one's own soul, and vice versa.

A world dominated by AI potentially reduces our human capacities by taking over more and more decisions and actions for us and by suggesting that humans are just machines controlled by a brain. A warm and loving human being on the other hand is able to empathically feel the need and pain of the other person and support her or him by just listening and being there. Machines are great if they take over routine tasks from us. AI is able to free us from those routine tasks and allows us to use our time and skills for creativity, innovation, arts and culture, and servicing and helping those who are in need of support and healing. How can we further strengthen and develop this growing autonomy? This question leads us to the next chapter about self-development and self-leadership, as a preparation for leadership in groups and organisations.

5.
Self-Leadership

5.1 A second enlightenment?

During the last 2,500 to 3,000 years humans have developed into increasingly autonomous beings. We emancipated from our natural environments such as our land, our families, and tribes. And during the last 400 years humanity developed towards what is called the age of enlightenment. The age of enlightenment is the intellectual and philosophical movement that dominated the world of ideas in Europe since the 16th century and has spread all over the world. Today we also call this the scientific revolution.

During this time, we have learned to think rationally and use logic. We have developed science. Our worldview is now based on subject and object. With this rational, logical, and materialistic way of thinking we are on an ending path, I believe. We use the resources of our earth several times. Climate change is already a fact and we need to adapt. What follows from this is that the world today is no longer in all aspects the world we want to have. The damaged environment and climate change are two prominent examples for this. It seems that we have lost the connection of our innovations with our core human values, such as love, care, truth, good judgement, ethics, justice, beauty, goodness, abundance – and the meaning we derive from following these values. It leads me to ask myself: can we solve these huge problems with the same thinking that created them?

I believe that we need additional qualities to pure rational and logical thinking. I believe we need to feel again what we think. We need to make use of our hearts, in addition to our heads. We need heartfelt thinking and service, and mindful action. We need to look at humans not only as having a body. We need to consider humans being spiritual beings with an "I" and a soul, I believe. According to the age of enlightenment, spirit and soul do not exist. Only matter exists. If we continue on this path, we will not be able to find the best solutions to our problems, I am afraid.

Recently I learned about a movement called Post-Materialistic Science. The scientists of this movement research the so-called paranormal phenomena. In Wikipedia we read: "Parapsychology is the study of paranormal and psychic phenomena, including telepathy, precognition, clairvoyance, psychokinesis, near-death experiences, synchronicity, reincarnation, apparitional experiences, and other paranormal claims. It is considered to be pseudoscience by a vast majority of mainstream scientists."

According to the Post-Materialistic Scientists these paranormal phenomena have been proved to be true. A vast amount of peer-reviewed studies supports this claim.[23] In what is called the Galileo Report[24], some of those scientists write that it is not matter which creates consciousness. Consciousness, they conclude, is first, and consciousness creates soul and matter. In point 13, of 14 argument points, they write: "Integrating an enlarged view of consciousness into science will also yield a new methodology that will have to be developed: the methodology of radical introspection or inner experience in which matter and mind, consciousness and its physical substrate, are two aspects of reality that are irreducible and simultaneously occurring perspectives

---

23   http://library.noetic.org/library/publication-articles/selected-peer-reviewed-journal-publications-psi-research.
24   See the Galileo Report at the end of this book.

of an underlying reality to which we otherwise have no direct access." In my own words paragraph 13 advises us to use our consciousness, or mind, or thinking, not only for matter, but also for introspection and inner experiences, for soul and spirit. This creates a new view on earth, humans, and the cosmos. It would allow me, without losing scientific ground, to use my thinking, my consciousness, to include not only matter, but also soul and spirit, into my realm of cognition. It would allow me to include in my thinking also feeling, and to consider the power within my mind, the willing, as explained earlier in this book. It would allow me to experience within my own consciousness my full humanity, my being fully human, including thinking, feeling, and willing.

I am enthusiastic about this Post-Materialistic Scientist movement. It allows for including matter, soul, and spirit into one worldview, by using what we have learned in the age of enlightenment: rational thinking and logic. But it requires that we are open for learning, open for an integrated worldview which includes matter, soul, and spirit. My enthusiasm grows when I think of quantum physics and quantum philosophy, which works with the concepts of non-locality and entanglement. This new and integrated worldview then includes local phenomena (matter), as well as non-local phenomena (soul and spirit). Deepak Chopra and Menas Kafatos even go so far to title their most recent book "You are the Universe". In it they summarise that consciousness is first, not matter, and that humans influence the universe with every feeling, thought, and action. They write: "We participate in the universe by finding order and figuring out where the patterns come from."[25]

I suggest to speak about the "1st enlightenment" instead of the

---

25 Chopra, Deepak and Kafatos, Menas: "You are the Universe." New York 2017

age of enlightenment, for the historic period of the last 400 years, in which we learned to think rationally and in subject-object separation terms. I then suggest to speak of a "2nd enlightenment", which is aiming for an integrated worldview, including matter, soul, and spirit. My feeling and hope is that we might be able to solve the huge challenges of our time with the help of such an integrated worldview. My hope would be that it should be possible to find solutions to our problems, because if consciousness is first and creates matter, then we should be able to learn how to use consciousness to influence and change matter. Whether at all and how this could be done of course needs further research.

The Galileo Report gives us a first idea what the 2nd enlightenment would entail. The quote above points to us developing a methodology of radical introspection or inner experience in which matter and mind, consciousness and its physical substrate, are only aspects of one integrated reality. The 1st enlightenment is teaching us only the physical substrate. The 2nd enlightenment teaches us to not only deal with the physical, but to include mind, consciousness, introspection, and inner experience into the realm of our perception, observation, and experience. I continue using the scientific, logical, and rational way of thinking. But I now include my heart within thinking. I include my feelings and my experiences, for finding best solutions.[26]

---

26 How the 2nd enlightenment may lead to us being able to influence and change matter through the proper use of introspection und using the heart and feelings, together with thinking, is the topic of many other books (for instance: Goswami, Amit (PHD): "The Everything Answer Book. How quantum science explains love, death and the meaning of life"), and research papers. As an introduction one may read the science of the heart as can be found on the website of www.heartmath.com. Also check their research regarding the Global Coherence Project. The research of the HeartMath Institute points to the interconnectednes of all things by using the heart as a sensory organ.

Based on my suggestion to introduce and speak about the age of the 2nd enlightenment I would now like to turn the attention to the harmonious human being, to myself and to you, the other person. Radical introspection is being done mostly alone. The question arises: how can I relate to you? How can I overcome my being alone?

One way for me to relate to you can be my interest in you. If I am interested in you, I will ask questions and will listen with empathy. These three,

1. my interest in you,
2. my questions to you, and
3. my empathic listening to what you say,

are strong forces to go the way from being alone towards being together, to team and community. If I ask you with interest and empathy: who are you and who do you want to become? – you most probably will be fully present and conscious, trying to give me an authentic answer. Your true self may appear. But for this you need me, the one who asks such a question. If we both do this to each other, we can share our interests, our ambition, and our challenges. And our challenges have a lot to do with our feelings. During a normal day we have positive and negative feelings. Feelings strongly influence our performance and our ability to socialise with others. For this reason, I will focus in this chapter on feelings and provide some tools for how to deal with them. By putting together some of those tools my intention is to support the view that we can purify our emotions and feelings and are able to create harmony in our soul. This harmony in my own soul forms a good basis for cooperation with others, and for building high-performance teams.

5.2 Creating harmony in the soul

The soul, I suggested, includes thinking, feeling, and willing. When we talk about the soul we naturally speak predominantly about our feelings. Soul moments can appear when we experience or do something together. Good business practices are based on good relationships. Good relationships include empathy and interest for the other person's needs. This is a soul quality. I am able to feel how the other person is and what she needs. This then leads to ideas and actions to serve her. In our modern, self-constructed world, often, the human soul is not cared for well enough. The human soul is drying out. Then negative soul moments can happen. We get angry at someone's words or actions. We do not like someone. We criticise ourselves. We blame others.

The soul is appearing and disappearing every moment during the day. The soul allows us time for reflection and recreation. For this I need to be present in the moment of time. The soul allows me to ask questions and not to expect an answer immediately. Especially difficult questions need time to find their answers and I can create soul moments of quiet reflection for those difficult questions. I can take time to let some preliminary answers appear. I can do this in dialogueue with others. Together we find better solutions to difficult questions.[27]

Self-development and self-leadership take place in our partnerships and family, and at the workplace. Self-leadership for me means to create harmony and balance within thinking, feeling, and willing so that I am able to use my skills for fulfilling my life's goal and for serving others. In meeting others my own soul appears, my strength and areas for improvement become visible to others and to me. It is the way I feel which determines

---

27 These reflections about the soul are inspired by Adriaan Bekmans book "Die menschliche Schöpfung" (English title "The Human Creation"), Borchen 2018.

my performance in such situations. If I feel well centred and in coherence, I may be a blessing to others and may perform well. If I feel unhappy, empty from inside, tired, or stressed, I may create stress for others, resulting in lower performance.

Therefore, my question is: how do I create harmony in my soul. How do I learn to better deal with my lower emotions, like stress or shame, and learn to use them with benefits, and transform them into higher emotions, for the purpose of being better able to serve others?

I believe we need more leaders who are able to facilitate teams which are dealing openly not only with emotions and challenges, but also with the complex issues of our time. We need leaders, I believe, who are taking up one of the most challenging question of today: how do we align artificial intelligence with human values? In order to be able to deal with this question leaders need to be able to connect with their own feelings, with themselves, and need to be able to create a certain degree of harmony in their souls.

In her book "Daring Greatly: How the Courage to Be Vulnerable Transforms the Way We Live, Love, Parent, and Lead"[28] Brené Brown writes about shame: "We all have it. Shame is universal and one of the most primitive human emotions that we experience. The only people who don't experience shame lack the capacity for empathy and human connection"... "We are all afraid to talk about shame. The less we talk about shame, the more control it has over our lives." Shame is the fear of disconnection, because we have done something wrong, or we have failed to live up to our own ideal or the ideal of others. It leads to the feeling that I am not worthy or good enough for love, belonging, or connection. It leads to the feeling that I am

---

28   Brown, Brené: Daring Greatly: "How the Courage to Be Vulnerable Transforms the Way We Live, Love, Parent, and Lead", New York 2012

unlovable, that I am flawed, that I am wrong. Shame comes when our business gets into bankruptcy, or when my boss is calling me an idiot in front of the client, or when my partner is leaving me for another, better, one. Shame is real pain.

Shame is one of several lower emotions which drag your feelings even further down. Other such emotions are fear, stress, anxiety, frustration, anger, sadness, grief, despair, loneliness, envy, suffering, adversity, illness, fear of death, complaining, blaming. According to the research done by David R. Hawkins[29] emotions can be put on an energy-scale between 0 and 1,000, whereby the lower emotions range below 200, and the higher emotions range above 200. The research is based on thousands of calibrations drawn from kinesiologic testing of individuals. The exact description of the method of testing can be found in the book. Here I only want to provide the result of this research. It is summarised in what Hawkins calls the Map of Consciousness. It shows that shame belongs to the lowest emotions and has an energy-level of 20. Guilt has an energy-level of 30, apathy 50, grief 75, fear 100, desire 125, anger 150, pride 175, and courage 200.

As Hawkins describes, with the help of courage we are able to turn things into the positive. If I have the courage to admit my shame, to speak to others about it, to be willing to work with it and get over it, then I am able to develop higher emotions. These higher emotions are, according to Hawkins: neutrality 250, willingness 310, acceptance 350, reason 400, love 500, joy 540, peace 600, enlightenment 700 – 1,000. The higher the energy level, the stronger the effect of your emotional state on others and on the environment around you.

Hawkins calls this the map of consciousness because he attaches to these emotions a characterisation of the consciousness

---

29 Hawkins, David R.: "Power vs. Force. An Anatomy of Consciousness. The Hidden Determinants of Human Behaviour." New York 2012

attached to the emotion. For instance, with shame a process of elimination is attached. With guilt – destruction. With fear – withdrawal. With anger – aggression. With courage – empowerment. With willingness – intention. With reason – abstraction and analysis. With love – revelation and forgiveness. With joy – transfiguration. With enlightenment – pure non-local consciousness and connectedness.

I am aware that this would need more explanation. I like the idea that there are lower emotions which we can take as messengers for us to learn, and that there are higher emotions and feelings which bring us in harmony with ourselves and the world around us.

During my more than 20 years of professional work in banking and finance I have given money to many people and teams. The successful individuals and teams were able to deal with their lower emotions and conflicts in a productive way. They had a positive approach to conflict. They found ways to confront themselves and others. They had good processes of finding the right people and of saying goodbye to those whose behaviour did not fit. The less successful individuals and teams were not able to deal with conflicts properly. They were not able to confront themselves with their own lower emotions and areas for behavioural improvement. In observing how the investments and loans I had provided developed over time I could see how dealing with emotions and conflict, which influenced behaviour, was one of the main factors for business and financial success.

I want to take another angle to dealing with emotions and consider the three soul-capacities of thinking, feeling, and willing, and observe their counterparts: being judgemental, being cynical, and being afraid.[30]

Being judgemental means that I would judge somebody by just

---

30   Scharmer, Otto: "Theory U", San Francisco 2009

seeing him or her without really looking with interest and empathy. I can also imagine two people who know each other for many years. They have developed a habit of judging each other like: each time you say this it feels to me like I am being judged.

Being cynical would be for instance when the younger generation comes up with a new idea and the older expert says: "Ah, that does not work, we have tried this already 20 years ago." And he would say this with some contempt in his voice.

Being afraid is trickier. We all have many fears which we are not always conscious of. It can mean for instance that someone in the room blamed an innocent person and nobody speaks up. They let it pass and the lie is now there, in the heart of all of them, and most hurtful, in the heart of the non-guilty, but wrongly blamed person. The fear of losing my job, or to speaking up against the boss, prevented me from making transparent that the blamed person is actually innocent.

Brené Brown describes sixteen armoured behaviours and contrasts them with what she calls daring behaviour. I find this a very helpful list of tools to work with, when dealing with my emotions, and with those of others.[31]

With mindfulness, loving care for myself, and attention, with taking notice of those emotions, I can transform them into higher, more purified emotions. Another way to describe this process could be: by learning to accept my lower emotions I am better able to focus on harmony and higher emotions. This is not easy. It is sometimes very, very difficult. If I am not careful enough, I will go to positive emotions too fast. Then I might not notice that deep down my fear, or shame, or pain, is still there.

---

31   Brown, Brené: "Daring Greatly: How the Courage to Be Vulnerable Transforms the Way We Live, Love, Parent, and Lead" New York 2012: For instance, her number 8 armoured behaviour is "Hiding Behind Cynicism." And the corresponding daring leadership behaviour is "Modeling Clarity, Kindness and Hope".

Then true transformation will not be possible. Am I able to reach down to the deepest layers of my own soul and find out about my pain and shame there?

To do this, I believe, we need to like ourselves, to love ourselves, to become the best friend of ourselves. How do we build a good, friendly, and loving relationship with ourselves? How do we become our own best friend? For this, we need attention, awareness, acceptance, and forgiveness. We tend to expect from others to make us happy. But how about that it is only me who is able to make me happy? When was the last time I asked myself how I am, how do I feel? When was the last time that I had an intimate conversation with myself? A good, partnering relationship with myself is of key importance for any relationship with others and for good leadership.

Many people do not take care of themselves well enough. I had to learn this the hard way myself and had to go through two burn-outs. And still I am not good enough yet with taking good care of myself and sensing my needs when I should. Recently I have started to use the morning time to take the care I need for myself. I then get up at 5.00 a.m. in the morning, or 5.30, and use two hours only for myself. During this time, I talk to myself as a good friend would talk to me. I reflect on what has happened during the last days and how I am going to deal with it. I try to notice how my soul is feeling, whether there are any pains or fears I need to deal with, or any situations I need to forgive myself and others. I then read about the process of forgiveness, I read about how to learn to love myself. This morning-time can also be time for some exercise, some music or arts, and some reflective and soul-nourishing reading. It can be time for deep meditation and prayer.[32] I know, I can do this work with myself

---

32 The morning routine is inspired by the book "Miracle Morning" by Hal Elrod, 2016

d still behave badly the next moment. This is human nature. ut over time I believe I can get better in small and humble steps. When I build such a relationship with myself, I will also discover my shadow sides, especially when I take note of when I blame others. Blame towards others is always a good start to ask myself what my problem is, instead of his or her problem. Or I look for critical feedback from others to reflect on my areas for improvement. Shadow-work makes me more realistic about my own strength and weaknesses. I can practise forgiveness towards my own weaknesses. I can also look at the shadows of others and practise forgiveness for them. It helps me to make more realistic and fair judgements about the skills and perseverance of others. I have seen many business plans during my time as fund- and credit manager in finance and banking. Many of those business plans are too illusionary and do not take into account the difficulties on the way. When those difficulties came it was mostly based on overconfidence of the persons involved. They would overestimate their own skills. Or they would end up in conflicts and not being aware enough of their own shadows.

I am potentially able to find the courage for taking full responsibility for my life and anything which comes towards me. I am potentially able to accept and to understand why things are as they are, and why people are as they are. This understanding may create feelings of appreciation and love for them. In many cases it is better to ask why someone behaves and acts like she or he does, instead of judging and criticising. Then feelings of acceptance, reflection and reason, love, joy, peace, and enlightenment, may potentially appear. Then individual and team performance can potentially increase.

On this way to creating harmony in the soul, things like affirmations, forgiveness, and meaning, may be of help. But this will only work if I am able to reach down to my lower emotions and find a way to understand why I have them and how they are related to my specific life situation. One way to connect to my emotions is to notice my body and look for stiffness or pains which might point me to underlying emotions and soul-pains.

I will describe six concepts which I find helpful for creating harmony in the soul. I choose those six because for me they have been most effective in dealing with some of my own issues. There are many other similar tools in modern teachings and literature, and I can only encourage the reader to look around and find those that work best for your own and your teams and partners' issues.

As a basis for this work I suggest to regularly use the HeartMath Coherence exercise which I mentioned earlier. Why? Because this exercise creates a certain base line of quietness, heart focus and calmness, for your work with yourself:

1. Focus on your heart area;
2. Breathe gently in and out through the heart area;
3. Generate and radiate a feeling of appreciation, gratitude or love; you can do this by imaging a happy moment in your life, or a beautiful place in nature, or a person you love, and feel and radiate the love.

5.2.1 Work with pain and fear

The **first concept** is by Dr Edith Eva Eger. I am very impressed by the story of her and how she survived the Holocaust. Her whole life after her surviving she was actively looking to face her deepest fears, one after the other. In her book "The Choice" she describes how she dealt with them, how she could heal herself, until she finally claimed freedom for herself.[33] At the end of her book she proposes eight steps which she learned during her life journey as being helpful. Those eight steps, as I read them, are:

---

33   Eger, Edith Eva, Dr: "The Choice". New York 2017

1. Notice the pain, the feeling;
2. Accept it;
3. Check body reaction (sometimes in extreme cases the body can react in an extreme way and you maybe need medical help immediately);
4. Stay; this step is very important; stay in the pain for so long until it changes or until it goes away; this may take a few months; you can also put a question into this step like: What do I really need?
5. What do you want (use your brain, think, strategise, make a plan)?
6. Who wants it (be sure that you do not follow "old" loyalties to others, marriage partner, boss, parents, those who punished you, etc., it must be your true self who wants it)?
7. What are you going to do about it (action, consider the risks involved)?
8. When? And then do it.

What I like about these eight steps is that from step 1. to 4. I really deal with the emotion, with the pain. I stay. That requires a lot of courage and persistence. I can do this every day again and again by sitting down, envisioning my pain, going into it, feeling it, suffering from it – so long, until the pain transforms and until my "pain-muscle" has grown so much that the pain may still be there, but that it will not have control over me anymore. Some might ask: why should I put myself again and again into the same pain? Because, only when I do it again and again will it transform, and will I gain the strength to have control over it.

When I feel that it has transformed, I am ready for step 5 and to use my thinking. Step 6 is also good in checking again that it is really me who wants it and that I from now on really live my own life, not the life of others anymore. And step 7 and 8 are about willing and action. Here it is helpful to consider the risks involved. You might want to speak to somebody now or confront somebody. But you do not know how she or he will react. This is a risk to consider. The first four steps deal with emotion, step 5 – 7 deals with thinking, and step 8 deals with willing. So, all three soul qualities are being addressed with this 8-step-process.

This example shows to me, how transformation of difficult emotions is only possible when I am willing and able to face the pain and fear, dive into it, stay with it, until it changes and transforms. This trains the "I", becoming stronger, more able to face difficulties. And with a stronger "I" I am potentially better able to deal with my own shortcomings, accept them with mindfulness and compassion, and do my best to get better next time.

5.2.2 Eight pillars of joy

The **second concept** is from the "Book of Joy" by Dalai Lama and Bishop Tutu.[34] In the end of the book they describe an 8-step meditation process about how to deal with lower emotions and pain and how I can train to strengthen my emotional muscle so that they lose control over me. The process is as follows: I look at a painful experience or emotion, I put it into my soul, into my focus. I feel the pain, shame, guilt, fear, or anger. I imagine the event when it happened vividly. And then I add a little of each of the eight ingredients to the event:

---

34   Dalai Lama, Bishop Tutu: "The Book of Joy", 2016

1. **Perspective** – broaden the perspective a bit; take out a bit of significance;
2. **Humility** – realise that we are not alone in our pain;
3. **Humour** – cultivate and use a smile, do not take yourself too seriously;
4. **Acceptance** – meditate about the current moment, be fully present, without judgement or expectations, give it some context and meaning;
5. **Forgiveness** – learn how to forgive, study and exercise the process of how to forgive in view of your pain, forgive yourself first, then others;
6. **Gratitude** – realise the daily small and bigger blessings of life and what others give to you;
7. **Compassion** – cultivate compassion in view of your pain;
8. **Be generous** – give and help others on the body, soul, and spirit level; be generous to yourself first; feel the deep generosity in your heart, then extend this feeling to others.

My own experience is that if I do this regularly, over time more joy is coming into my life. In the book the exercise is ending with the encouragement to celebrate!

5.2.3 Ho'oponopono

The **third concept** for dealing with emotion is an old Hawaiian wisdom verse, called Ho'oponopono: "I am sorry; please forgive me; I love you; thank you". My experience with working and meditating these four sentences is a very warm and healing one. I think about an issue I have with someone, or something I did or said to someone which I feel sorry about, or something painful someone did to me. I imagine what happened in a clear and colourful image, and then I meditate the four lines. It creates a healing atmosphere around the issue. Sometimes it can be experienced that immediately the issue changes, the people involved react differently, the situation is part of the good life process again. The four lines can be used in any following order, for instance like this: I love you, please forgive me, I am sorry, thank you. Or like this: I am sorry, please forgive me, thank you, I love you. I feel the difference of each version and use it differently for each of the issues at hand.

I recommend reading the literature about it in order to better understand where these lines come from and how they can be best used, for instance "Zero Limits" by Joe Vitale.[35] In my travels and courses, I sense that these four lines are being used by many people all over the world.

5.2.4 Love for no reason

The **fourth concept** for dealing with emotions is from Marcy Shimoff in her book "Love for No Reason". She describes the seven chakras in relation to love for no reason.[36] Here is a brief summary of her concept:

---

35 Joe Vitale: "Zero Limits: The Secret Hawaiian System for Wealth, Health, Peace, and More", New York 2007
36 Shimoff, Marci. "Love For No Reason: 7 Steps to Creating a Life of Unconditional Love "(p. 156). Atria Books. Kindle-Version

1. **Safety** – Being in the Here and Now. Your connection to Mother Earth, the physical world, and your material life. Get grounded, plant yourself in the present moment. Sense your support, inner security.
2. **Vitality** – Turning up the juice. Give your body true nourishment. Supply your love-body with high quality fuel. Eat, breathe, exercise and delight, increase your Prana, your life force. Feel and experience your feelings directly and completely instead of suppressing or venting them.
3. **Unconditional Self-Love** – Loving Yourself No Matter What. Your connection to your sense of self, your will, and your authentic power. Love the unlovable in yourself: practise self-compassion, self-forgiveness, and self-acceptance to bring the vibration of love to your own being, just as you are. Honour your Power: take responsibility for your own experience of life and love.
4. **Openness** – Living with an Open Heart. Your connection to others and the world. Give from Fullness: expand your heart by being compassionate, kind, altruistic, and forgiving. Give what you have and not more. Let Love In: boost your ability to receive love through practice; make a habit of gratitude, appreciation, and opening your heart through awe and "aaahhh".
5. **Communication** – Coming from Compassion. Your connection to your speech, your expression, and your ability to hear others. Speak the language of love: express yourself as an agent of love, communicating what's true for you, including your feelings and needs.

> Hear from the heart: listen empathetically ally for the subtext – what's really being said beneath others' words.
> 6. **Vision** – Seeing with the eyes of love. Your connection to your inner wisdom, your intuition, beauty, and truth. Look for the beauty: see the perfection in imperfection and recognise the same spirit in everyone. Trust your inner Wisdom: pay attention to your heart's promptings, which come to you as inner knowing or flashes of intuition.
> 7. **Oneness** – connection to wholeness. Your connection to wholeness, grace, and the Divine. Plug in to presence: tune your "satellite dish" to the Divine by making time for stillness. Meditate or pray each day – especially in the morning. Surrender to Grace: let go and trust the universe to put you in the right place at the right time.

One simple way of dealing with these 7 levels of love and self-love is to just read them every day. When I do this for some time, I feel that I have more awareness for these seven areas, that I am better able to notice from which level I am currently acting. Is it the very human but needy area of the lower chakras, or is true open-heart unconditional love, inspired by the higher chakras? It also helps me to harmonise my soul. As Marci Shimoff writes: "As the fourth of the seven chakras, the heart centre sits in the middle of the chakra system. It's seen as a meeting point or bridge: the place where the integration of mind and body, or spirit and matter, happens. It's where the earthly (the lower three chakras) and the divine (the upper three chakras) marry. When your heart chakra is open, life 'comes together' for you. You can handle both the physical side of life (money, job, health) and the spiritual side (your life's purpose, wisdom, and connection to the divine), while still staying firmly anchored in the energy of love."[37]

5.2.5 Reflecting on your day with inner calmness

The **fifth concept** to support creating harmony in the soul is to reflect on your emotions and behaviour in the evening shortly before going to sleep. It is inspired by Rudolf Steiner's book "Knowledge of Higher Worlds".[38] Look at your day and see yourself from the outside, like others have seen you during the day, or like you would look at you from a hill. Reflect on the events of the day and on your emotions related to those events. Try to make sense of them, to recognise links and meanings. And imagine how you would have acted if you had been in better synchronisation with your higher Self, your highest hopes, your highest ideals. If I do that every day, I notice how my life subtly changes and how I am better able to lift myself up to more purified emotions and ideals.

5.2.6 Six heart qualities

The **sixth and final concept** to support creating harmony in the soul is also inspired by Rudolf Steiner. He has mentioned it in several of his books and lectures, for instance in his book "Occult Science".[39]

---

[37] Shimoff, Marci. "Love For No Reason: 7 Steps to Creating a Life of Unconditional Love" (p. 156). Atria Books. Kindle-Version.
[38] Steiner, Rudolf: "Knowledge of Higher Worlds", https://www.rsarchive.org/GA/index.php?ga=GA0010
[39] Steiner, Rudolf: "Occult Science", https://www.rsarchive.org/GA/index.php?ga=GA0013

There are five heart qualities, or soul-skills, that can be of help in creating harmony in your soul. The five heart qualities are five exercises which are complemented by a sixth exercise. The five exercises are to train your thinking, willing, feeling, the choice for the positive, and openness or lifelong learning. The last and sixth exercise would be to perform these five all together all the time during the day.

First, train for the ability to focus and concentrate on your thinking. Our smartphones and the many different chats constantly interrupting us are one of the adversaries of focus, concentration, and what experts call deep work (see the book by Cal Newport: Deep Work).

The exercise can be done in many different ways. Take a simple thought, like "wisdom lives in light", and reflect about it for a few minutes. Put only related thought after thought to it. Or take the image of a red square and a blue square, filled with those colours. The red square is on top, the blue square below. Now change that. Move the blue square on top and the red square below. Can you do it? Or take a circle filled with red colour. Then, starting from the middle, a small blue dot emerges and becomes bigger and bigger until the whole red circle is filled with blue. The blue pushes away the red. Then, starting from the middle, a small red dot emerges and becomes bigger and bigger, until the whole blue circle is filled with red. And now do it backwards. Or take a pen and reflect about its size, colour, materials, its way from raw materials to production, to the shop, and into your hand. Just be sure you put one thought after the next, each one thought logically following out of the previous thought and try not to diverge into daydreaming.

Second, train your willing. This one is a bit more difficult. It is about doing what you say or doing what you have put yourself as a goal. To most effectively train your will, it is best to choose simple tasks which do not involve any motivation for doing it.

You can choose to lift your arm at a set time of the day. It is important to set such time, remember it when the time arrives, and lift your arm. Or you choose to tip with your hand three times on your leg. It should be an action which carries no sense or meaning at all. This is because then nothing else is motivating your action and you can be sure to perform a free act out of free choice and will. The thing is, you will most probably forget it when the time arrives. Let's say you choose at 8 a.m. today to lift your arm at 10 a.m. today. Most probably you will forget. At noon or so you remember. Then do it! And feel the positive energy of doing a free act of will, despite that you missed the right time. Over time you will remember better. This exercise also creates a new consciousness about time. Over time you will notice that you do not need to look at your watch so often anymore because your time-feeling has improved so that you pretty well know how late it is during the day.

Third, train to be able to express your feelings as you wish. Often, we are expressing our feelings directly, either in tears or in aggression. The goal of the exercise is to be able to control the expression of your feelings. Do not control your feelings themselves. They should be noticed with attention and mindfulness, with love and care. They should be fully acknowledged, felt, and accepted. The exercise is about the expression of those feelings. It may well be that you want to shout or show your deep sadness: in such cases show it consciously and with mindfulness regarding the expression and the choosing of your words. Try to put some distance and freedom of choice between the immediate feeling and your reaction to it. This exercise is difficult to do during a set time. You can do it all day. Remember it and practise it all the time. Your feelings will not become dull and faint. On the contrary, your feelings will be noticed by yourself with more attention and loving care. If you feel sad, you feel it full-heartedly. The only thing is: if you express it, try to express it with mindfulness in regard to the other person, and for yourself. We all know that harsh words against others will hurt them and will also hurt ourselves. Because afterwards, we may feel sorry. This exercise helps you to express your feelings in a more balanced way.

Fourth, train the ability to see shadows, but decide for the light, to see evil, but decide for the good, to see failure, but decide for success. How often do we complain about others? In those cases, try to understand why the other person is like he or she is. If you understand, accept. You can anyway only change yourself, and not others. And then decide to look for the positive sides in the other person and focus on those. Try to do so with anything which comes on your way and which appears negative. Think about world politics. Enough reason to blame politicians that they do not care enough for climate change. Then understand, how a myriad of commercial interests may block wise political decisions. Then go further and look for all the positive initiatives in the world that fight against climate change. And maybe even change your own behaviour and save some waste, or energy, or the likes. This exercise helps you to come into the habit of a positive approach to any challenge you are faced with. It will enable you to see the challenges, see the limitations and shadows, but you decide and make a choice for the positive.

Fifth, train openness and lifelong learning. Try to avoid thoughts like: "Ah, I know this already. Nothing will change anyway. I have seen it happen and it will not work." Stay always open to new things. Learn lifelong. Read a lot and constantly learn new things. If you are not a reader than ask good questions to anybody you meet and keep learning. This exercise helps you never to stop learning and developing.

Sixth, try to do these exercises all together all the time. You might want to start by doing the first exercise for a month, then the second for a second month. After five months you could start combining them during the day. And before the year ends you are doing them all the time, every day.

My own experience of exercising them since many years is that they will be a great help to create a resilient and harmonious emotional and soul-life.

5.3 Leadership evolution

A helpful way of understanding how to develop yourself can be described as leadership evolution. It is inspired by the book of Alan Watkins: Coherence.[40] I believe that this concept gives some direction towards where leadership evolution could go, towards what kind of goals I might want to strive for. Watkins suggests the following development steps (shortened list, see his book for a detailed description):

- Impulsive;
- Ego-centric;
- Self-protective;
- Conformist;
- Expert;
- Achiever;
- Pluralist;
- Integrator;
- Magician;
- Unitive.

40 Watkins, Alan: "Coherence", London 2014

Most people today are challenged to become team leaders, coming from the development state of being experts in their fields. I have seen this typically happen in automotive firms like Audi, or Mercedes. The engineer, who has learned and studied to build the best fossil fuel motors, all of a sudden finds him- or herself in the position of team leader or department leader. Now he needs to deal with people's issues and has never learned it. He needs to develop from expert to achiever and to integrator, in order to be able to integrate different opinions and individuals of his team into one common goal.

To develop into an integrator, and further into a magician, requires broadening my interest and worldview. I need to learn to integrate different and diverse opinions, characters, cultures, and behaviours. A magician as the next step of leadership evolution would be someone who listens long and deep, and when he finally speaks his words will have a strong impact. Think of people like Nelson Mandela, or Martin Luther King and their strong and "magical" impact on millions of people.

In leadership trainings, I put an effort into such understanding of self-development as a basis for the development of true team and community leadership qualities.

5.4 The "I" appears in the soul

What do I mean with "The 'I' appears in the Soul?"

I remember once that I was very tired and also a bit ill. I was in a meeting, drifting away. All of a sudden, the leader of the meeting asked me directly and without further notice: Alexander, tell us a bit about how you deal with money in your personal and professional affairs. This call on me immediately woke me up completely. I was fully present within a fraction of a second, sweating. Everyone in the room was looking at me. And I began telling my story.

This is an example of how the other person calls upon you, asks you a waking-up-question, and as a result, your "I" appears, meaning: you are now fully conscious and present. When the "I" is present, I am present. I am fully aware that I am here in the Now. I know what I am saying or doing. I act with consciousness.

This is not always the case. Often during the day, we are in a dreamier state of being, not fully conscious and not fully present in the moment. When we are not conscious, our shadow sides of our souls are potentially there to appear. In such a case I might say harsh words to my business partner or spouse, which afterwards I might regret.

From another angle we speak of our ego, or self, which represents our daily needs, and we can speak of our higher Self (capital S), which represents our highest hopes, our mission in life. When I connect to my highest hopes, I can choose to look back at my day, or the last week, and reflect on it. I can make a judgement about whether my actions were in line with my purpose. When I do this, I call upon my higher Self, my higher "I", for presence, conscience, and good judgement.

This higher Self reaches beyond the soul with thinking, feeling, and willing. It reaches into the realm of the spirit, where the ideals, the universal laws exist. Each of us is able to reach into that big sea of ideas and concepts. From here, I believe, all the great works of arts, technology, innovation, and spiritual development are coming.

In his book "The Way of the Seal Mark Divine" offers a great list of questions, which one could use in daily reflection, and which involve asking about my purpose, which is connected to my higher Self. He calls it Morning Routine and Evening Ritual[41]:

---

41 Divine, Mark: "The Way of The Seal", New York 2015, pp. 232 and 233

- What and whom am I grateful for today?
- What am I excited about and looking forward to doing today?
- What is my purpose, and do my plans for today connect me to it?
- How can I move the dial toward my goals today?
- To whom can I reach out and serve or thank today?
- Are my goals still aligned with my purpose?

When I am doing this morning routine for myself, I can feel how some of these questions really lift me up, help me in getting more conscious about what I really want in life, help me calling upon my "I" within my soul.

The morning routine is complemented with an Evening Ritual:

- Was I "on" and in the zone today or "off" and unbalanced?
- What contributed to that feeling?
- What were the top three positive things I accomplished or that happened today? What did I learn from them?
- Are there unsolved challenges I would like my subconscious mind to help me solve tonight?
- What went wrong today and what is the silver lining?

For me there are two key elements in this evening ritual. One is the question: Was I "on" or "off"? For me this means: Was my "I" present, was I fully present in the moment, was I conscious about my true purpose, and acting accordingly, or not? The other key element for me is the suggestion to use the subconscious mind to help me solve unsolved challenges. Here Mark Divine suggests using the wisdom of the night, the wisdom of the universe, to which we all potentially have access, for finding some answers to unsolved challenges.

In my understanding it is the "I" which has access to the wisdom of the universe. Without the "I" present, the soul is without guidance and comes up with emotions, thoughts, and actions, in an uncontrolled way. With the "I" present, the soul has a direction. It is necessary to renew this direction every moment and to ask myself, whether I am still acting in line with my higher Self, my higher purpose. It is me myself who realises my own biography. In realising my own biography, I follow my interests. With interest flows warmth and love. With the warm and interested "I" I can get enthusiastic about an idea, a concept. This enthusiasm can create warmth and interest in others too and they also get enthusiastic. This enthusiasm is an important factor in motivating others.

It is the "I" which is able to reach into the realm of ideas and creation. This can also be called the realm of the spirit. Every human being is able to reach into that realm in every moment. It is a universally accessible world of concepts and eternal laws.

I suggest to look at the "I" as being inside and outside at the same time. In other words, the "I" represents a non-local presence. A local presence could only be in one place at the same time, not in two, or more places. Experience tells us that we are able to also communicate within this non-local realm. As the above-quoted intuition-research points us to, the heart has access to non-local information related to the future. This form of non-material interaction has been scientifically proved in many ways, as, for example, Goswami shows in his book.[42]

The concept of non-local, or non-material communication and interaction opens up a whole new world for us. It would allow us to integrate the spirit realm with the soul- and the material realm. From the spirit realm, as mentioned above, we are able to give meaning to our self-created organised world by reaching into the field of inspiring ideas and concepts. In social interaction we are able to integrate meaning and matter into relationship building. And in the material realm, the local-, or subject-object, world, we can integrate soul and spirit into the building of purposeful businesses and organisations.

To be conscious and present in the moment of time means to experience what I am thinking, feeling, and willing, while I am doing it. As a conscious human being I am able to know why I do things, and I can explain myself to others in a way they understand. With self-consciousness I am able to notice myself, to distance myself from myself, to become an observer of myself, to train myself certain skills, to become the best friend of myself. This is communication between the higher Self and the ego-self where the higher Self teaches, treats, forgives, and guides the ego-self through life and on the way to realise its own purpose.

I believe the human being exists because it wants to develop. We all want to get better at what we are doing. In most situations we are not only alone but also together with others. When I studied TheoryU with Otto Scharmer and 70 other participants during 2010 – 2012 in Boston and Berlin, I learned about the quote from Bill O'Brien, long-time CEO of Hanover Insur-

---

[42] Amit Goswami, PhD: "The Everything Answer Book. How Quantum Science explains Love, Death and the Meaning of Life", Charlottesville 2017

ance, who said: "The success of an intervention depends on the interior condition of the intervener." This quote impressed me a lot. I could see it immediately. The way I feel inside, the way I am connected with myself, effects my intervention outside.

In that sense leadership for me is first and foremost inner self-leadership, the ability to connect with yourself, to build a good, friendly and loving relationship with yourself. That provides then the basis for leading others, for developing leadership skills which enable me to lead teams and organisations. In the next chapter I will describe some aspects of how leadership can be implemented in organisations. I will also point to the other way of learning, not with self-love only, but together with others. Many issues we are facing today can only be solved together.

6.
Leadership in organisations

6.1 The vertical and the horizontal

In this chapter "Leadership in Organisations" I will point to some concepts of what can be called horizontal leadership and horizontal organising. Many of these concepts, which I will point to here, have been developed by Adriaan Bekman, founder of IMO Institute for Man and Organisationdevelopment.

Today there exist many new concepts of how to organise and lead: Self-Management, Democratic Leadership, Holacracy, Re-Inventing Organisations, Agile Leadership, TheoryU, Spiral Dynamics, and other similar concepts. All these concepts support the traditional hierarchical organisation to become more flexible. They support that people take up more responsibilities. And some of these concepts claim to abandon the hierarchy completely, like Self-Management.

In my experience any organisation has vertical *and* horizontal elements. It is one of the key leadership skills to be aware and able to act in good balance within both dimensions. Clients demand flexible organisations. The traditional hierarchy is often too slow to react flexibly and fast enough. Then more horizontal and flexible elements are necessary to be introduced. A traditional hierarchical organisation is being displayed in the vertical organisation chart with the CEO at the top. In such a model responsibilities and decision-making are established with a tendency towards the higher levels of the organisation. A horizontal organisation on the other hand will look more like a landscape of teams working together. Responsibilities are established with a tendency towards those places in the organisation where the client requires fast decision-making. Working in a horizontal way means that I involve my team as much as possible and with great transparency. Even in a self-managed organisation with no explicit vertical organisation structures there are still a lot of vertical elements existing, like responsibilities, or hierarchy based on experience, based on age, based on reputation, based on skills. Therefore, it is important to understand the concept and effects of vertical and horizontal leadership.

In a vertical organisation my job description is connected with my position within the hierarchy. The higher the position in the hierarchy the more responsibility is connected to the job. This model has the tendency that lower positions do not take the responsibility they should take. Instead they push decisions up in the hierarchy to higher levels. This often results in a certain complacency mood of employees which leave things up to the higher levels. Managers often feel the need to control most of the decisions. Such behaviour results in the higher levels having too many responsibilities and operational tasks on their desks. This leads them to spend too little time to take good care of their people, for strategy, for developing an efficient and motivating culture, and for giving meaning to the whole.

In horizontal leadership the aim is opposite to the vertical model. It is to bring down decision-making to those places in the organisation, where it deals with the client, and where fast decision-making with good service for the client is necessary. One of the main activities of top leaders will then not be to accumulate decision-making, but to bring decisions away from their own desk down to the levels and places where they belong – and then get out of the way! Such a leader will establish new processes that allow the lower levels to take up initiative and responsibility. Often people require more freedom and involvement in decision-making. But when it is really allowed and required some of those who wanted more responsibility struggle to really take the burden of the responsibility connected with it. Here the top leaders should support and enable them to grow and gain more courage and self-confidence.

Then they are able to take the necessary decisions themselves. Then the vertical hierarchy is amended with a landscape of flexible teams working together in many different ways. The hierarchy still exists but will be focusing more on enabling others. The horizontal landscape will develop parallel to the vertical structure with a broad variety of cooperation lines, teams, process owners, and activities, all focused on serving the client well.

On the way to a more horizontal way of working together many obstacles need to be overcome. Change is never easy. It follows from the image of the human being that some heart-related principles and ways of doing things become more relevant. If I have an image of the human being which is brain-focused I will naturally put logic first. I will try to use my best thinking skills to develop a smart plan. Then I will go into action and will try to realise that plan successfully, controlling every aspect of it on the way. Often during the day however, I do something without thinking about it beforehand. Afterwards I realise what I have done and analyse my action. First, we think, then we act. Or, first we act, and then we think. In the hectic of today's world these two ways are executed in a very fast way all the time. We have a brainstorm session, we develop some ideas, and we go into action immediately. We have a problem, we look for a solution, and act fast. Successful and fast implementation is one of the important ingredients of a successful business. According to the human being as described in the earlier chapter these two ways relate to the nerves and senses system and the metabolic limbs system only.

The threefold image of the human being however provides us

with a third system, the heart-and-rhythm system. Here the heart and breathing play their intermediating role. They allow us to breathe, to create space for calm reflection, for deep listening and dialogue. They allow us for vitalisation and refreshment. This points to a third way of approaching the world, which would integrate the first and second way mentioned. It would be to see and feel first, to sense with empathy, to listen well, to create a space for reflection, to ask enough good questions until things become really clear for everyone. This takes more time. True. Many in our fast-moving world would say "I have no time for this". But in such a process I can involve my team. I can listen to everyone carefully. I can let them speak. I can integrate different views. The chances for a better solution are very high because more people see more. With this I create a solid ground that everyone is involved and motivated, that everyone knows what to do and why. I create trust and coherence within the team. And then I realise the plan with empathy, constantly sensing whether my steps are still the right ones. And everyone feels involved and committed because everyone was part of designing the plan. My consciousness, or awareness, is now spread over a broader and fuller field of sensations, including feelings, soul, body movement, body reaction, and thinking, all related to myself and to others in the team. While I am actively doing things, I am at the same time in a sensing and listening, highly conscious mode. And I will be constantly asking others for feedback: am I still on the right track? I will also sense my own being and how I am. I will ask myself whether I am fresh enough for this task or whether I should take a short break. If everyone in a team is acting like this the team performs in unity and purposeful, in constant communication with each other, being fully aware of the strength and weaknesses of each other, being active, supportive, and receptive at the same time.

It seems to me that this way of working together is potentially more successful. Many recent books describe this new way of working together, which is based on a fuller image of the human being, including not only thinking and willing, but also feeling.[43]

At IMO[44] many simple but very effective set of tools have been developed which follow the way of acting from the heart. They are summarised in three words:

Process – dialogue – biography/the next step.

A process starts with a question. In a dialogue the team exchanges the best ideas and comes to a next step. In this dialogue, we bring in our full human being including our feelings and emotions, our biography, our identity, our best skills, while at the same time accepting and dealing with our and others' weaknesses and strength.

6.2 Process – dialogue – biography/the next step

First, there is a question. A question represents a tension between something that is and something that should be but is not clear yet. For instance, we might feel that the organisation should become more flexible. But we do not yet know how we can achieve that. That would be a typical question.

Second, we get together with others in the organisation (or in a private setting, two people, or more) and discuss the question. We get into a horizontal dialogueue. Hierarchy should not play a role here. Everyone speaks up about the same amount of time. The talk is personal and authentic. We play no roles. We say what we feel and believe we could contribute to the overall goal.

---

43 See for instance Bekman 2016, Brown 2018, Coyle 2017, Divine 2014
44 IMO Institute for Man and Organisationdevelopment, www.hetimo.net, for more information about IMO see chapter "Horizontal Organising"

We bring in our whole personality and skill, our biography. That creates a diverse image of what is and what should be. The horizontal leader, which could be anyone in the team, then facilitates to find a common ground how to go forward, so that everyone feels included and can agree.

Third, we get into action and do the next step towards the anticipated goal. Later we start again with a next question, get into a dialogue, involve ourselves fully (biography) and do a next step. We do this all the time, every day. We adapt flexibly. We learn constantly. And by doing this, we achieve our goals stepwise, incrementally, and with everyone involved and motivated.

These three steps, a question which leads to a process, a dialogueue in which we bring in our full human being, and the next step of everyone involved can also be described in a slightly different way:

First, the question brings us together, creates a process. In horizontal leadership the process is a focus area. Everything happens not only in space but also in time. Many processes are not going well because people are not taking enough care of the processes involved.

Second, we dialogueue about it. We use our collective intelligence. Everyone potentially has the right answers, not only the top managers. And together we find better solutions than alone. We work with the assumption that the intelligence for the solution is "in the room". It is not with the consultant, or team leader, but both have the skills to facilitate a process through which the team finds a next step.[45]

Third, in the dialogue we bring in our biographies, we share stories, we make it personal. This can start with the top leader-

---

45 In horizontal leadership I prefer to work with the concept of the next step instead of trying to find solutions. Often solutions suggest that

ship team sharing amongst them some of their own stories, challenges, failures, biographical moments. That opens the scene also for the lower levels to share their stories. This sharing of stories and challenges increases the trust and respect for each other because now I can better understand why the other person is like she or he is. And with this the next step of action can be done with full heart and soul, feeling fully included, understanding why and the purpose, and feeling more responsible for the whole and for the others in the team.

Biography is the deeper part of us working together. If I share my own challenge and show openly how I struggle, then others may open up also. This takes a lot of courage. It makes everything personal again. We have learned to be objective in our judgement and to keep away our personal, subjective issues. In horizontal leadership we have to do the opposite: have the courage to show up, show yourselves, be honest about how you feel, share your vulnerabilities. This also leads to a different way of giving feedback. In teams with a high level of trust feedback is given in a more direct way, and all the time. It is more effective to give small little corrections and feedback throughout the day than giving feedback only once in the annual appraisal meeting. Such traditional annual appraisal meetings often create strong de-motivation and disappointment because of lack of appreciation by the leader. I recommend abandoning the annual appraisal meeting alltogether and learning the more direct and immediate way of giving feedback instead. It is much more effective and allows us to learn and grow everyday – and experience the joy of it. It allows us to develop our biography, to grow in life and as a person.

we are finished talking, leaving open too many things unclear. If we talk about the next step the approach is different. We do not expect to have found the final solution, but we go into action already, learn incrementally and improve with every step. In many situations this is more motivating and productive than working the concept of solutions.

Annually, or semi-annually you could use the time for a motivating development-talk with your people. One of my clients calls this meeting the "star-meeting". In a one-on-one meeting the stars, the high-points, the strength, of the person and her work are being discussed in a horizontal dialogue. This may lead to questions of further improvement, or adjustment of work-focus according to the skill development of the employee. It is focused on the positive sides and on the joy-factors related to work.

Such a "star-meeting" is a very good thing to balance out the constant and immediate feedback given during work, which can be hard sometimes. As is being mentioned in the literature pointing to this: we do the hard work together, we are here to solve hard and difficult problems for our clients.

This three-step-tool of process, dialogue, and biography/the next step, provides for a new way of working in teams, based on a fuller image of the human being. In the next chapter I will point to some elements of how horizontal organisations can be developed, and how they potentially serve customer demands faster and better than vertical organisations.

6.3 Horizontal leadership

The demand to change the way we run organisations is huge. I experience this every day in my work. People wish to be more involved. They want to take up more responsibility. They ask for a better explanation of the Why and purpose of the organisation. They want to understand the context in which the organisation is active. They are longing for meaning and self-development. This requires a new paradigm for management and leadership. It requires the humanising of our organisations. The new paradigm enables teams to adapt their products and services rapidly in order to meet the fast-changing demands of customers. It permits organisations to flourish in this new world. These organisations can be called horizontal organisations. Horizontal organisations require horizontal leadership. And that requires self-development and self-leadership.

Organisations must radically reinvent how they are organised and led, and embrace the most advanced leadership skills and techniques, in order to become more flexible and to better serve their customers. Organisations first and foremost exist because their customers pay for their products and services. How often have organisations forgotten about the customer and are mainly busy with internal affairs?

Horizontal organisations aim to implement the following principles:

- They develop smart and flexible strategies and think first and foremost from the perspective of their clients. A great part of the strategy is being developed by the teams themselves, often in good cooperation with their clients, and based on a strong purpose and understanding of the Why of the organisation.
- The organisation structure is being changed into a network of teams and individuals. The traditional hierarchy is being reduced. The organisation structure is formed around the need and service to customers. Decisions are mostly made directly by the teams who serve the customers.
- Internal processes are as flexible as possible, based on strong values, culture, and effective behaviours. This takes time to develop because people need to develop. It needs high attention and focus. In many organisations, which I see, this part is very weak.
- Leadership is being brought down from the top to

lower levels. It is distributed amongst many different roles and tasks. These roles and tasks are clear for everyone. Self-organised teams have a great amount of self-responsibility. They care for their own and for the new team members; they do their own feedback processes; they support each other in their individual development. They work with the concept of process owner (see below).

- HR-Instruments are changing. They are coming from building and cementing the hierarchical organisation, from traditional goal-focused agreements with individual employees, from supporting careers and salary systems within the hierarchy. All this needs to change towards team building, new forms of daily feedback, designing team-oriented salary structures, supporting clarity of roles and responsibilities, and offering opportunities for personal growth. HR will not produce anymore long job descriptions. Instead it will support employees themselves to write their own short, half-page, description of task, responsibility, and accountability, as well as decision-making competence, all in line with the overall purpose of the organisation.

- Horizontal organisations aim for living a trustful culture. They focus on building such a culture. They know how difficult this is and pay special attention to it. Financial information is transparent to all. Lifelong learning is part of the organisation and of the people working there. Decisions are being made there where it is the best for the client.

- They have a clear and participatory strategy and a

clear long-term goal, a mission which is able to motivate employees and clients.

- They have a good explanation for the Why of the organisation, which is alive and clear to anybody and on all levels in and of the organisation. The Why makes sense and gives meaning to the current and future state of the organisation, its market surroundings, and clients. The importance of this giving meaning is often underestimated. How often does the leadership tell us: sure we have a mission-statement! And when you then go deeper into the organisation, you find out that: yes they have it, but it is not alive anymore, it does not live in every employee anymore, it has dried out, it has actually been forgotten by most employees, it is not a burning and motivating factor anymore.

- The horizontal organisation also needs new financial reporting and steering instruments to give full transparency to the teams and their activities. Those new financial instruments need to provide the teams with relevant financial information so that they are able to plan for action and see the effect of their action immediately also in financial terms. Otherwise, they would act blindly, not precisely knowing about the financial effects of their service and products. It needs a skilled financial department with enough phantasy and motivation to develop such tools in service of full transparency. Then financial reporting instruments can become a tool for steering social and value creating processes.

- And finally, a horizontal organisation is a living organism, created and maintained by people and individuals who are living human beings. Human beings perform in a certain state of their own development and biography. In a similar way, organisations also develop over time and have their own development phases, for instance developing from a flexible and innovative pioneer organisation to a well-organised bureaucratic organisation, and later into a highly efficient integrated and team-oriented value creator.

Horizontal leadership is a new and comprehensive way of looking at organisations and the people working in it. This new methodology, including a number of the concepts and tools mentioned, has been founded in 2005 by Adriaan Bekman, together with Bernhard Kloke. They gave it the name IMO Institute for Man and Organisationdevelopment, because the methodology puts people first. As mentioned, many of the concepts have been developed by Adriaan Bekman. Their work is based on the work of, and cooperation with, Bernard Lievegoed, a Dutch psychologist, medical doctor and leadership consultant, who based many parts of his work on the work of Rudolf Steiner (1861 – 1925). Today, 2019, IMO represents more than 50 years of experience with consulting in many different types of organisations, including business and not-for-profit, and is present with local groups in nine countries, including China. IMO currently has more than 60 consultants in 9 countries serving more than 400 clients. It is a good practise that the IMO consultants constantly develop the concepts further and do related research together. See www.het-imo-net.

The following description of what horizontal leadership means is inspired by Hermanus Meijerink of IMO Brazil, and I thank him for his clear thoughts.

Horizontal leadership shows itself in its results: people that are joyfully willing and able to act autonomously, out of their own initiative within the mission and objectives of the organisation for the satisfaction of their client's needs. A horizontal leader leads in such a way that the employees take full responsibility for the process they are working on. He (including she) offers conditions and introduces processes for self-development and learning on the job. He inspires by explaining the wider context, by giving meaning, by making sense of the mission and objective of the organisation. He intervenes when necessary by dialogueuing with the employee and helping him or her to understand the necessary adjustments to the process or behaviour. This can be summarised in four core qualities of horizontal leadership: 1. Managing and steering; 2. Coaching and mentoring; 3. Inspiring; 4. Integrating and Intervening.

The horizontal leader will constantly strengthen his own capacity of observing the reality he is working in. This is done through interaction with his team and colleagues, and through good listening. It requires social and entrepreneurial skills. Different possibilities are investigated, risks are being analysed, and a next step is found that brings the organisation to its next level. Those steps are rather small than big. They are based on constant learning and adapting. Many small steps then make a big change.

The horizontal leader is able to facilitate effective meetings and actions of his teams. This skill is necessary on all levels. The horizontal leader needs to be able to encourage a diverse discussion in which everyone in the team speaks about roughly the same time (see Google's "Aristotle" Study).[46] He then is able to facilitate good summaries to which all can agree.

Horizontal leadership, therefore, creates space and processes in which people are able to act autonomously, take initiative,

---

46   What Google Learned From Its Quest to Build the Perfect Team – The New York Times 25/02/16

and connect well with each other. Only when a person is connected to the wider meaning of the organisation, when she and he understands the needs of the client, when she knows the whole story (transparency) and when she and he has the skill, capacity and free space to take initiative, only then change and innovation can happen. Horizontal leadership creates processes for teams and individuals to work autonomously. It forms the link between the teams and the wider context and meaning of client and company. Today everyone is a leader in his and her circle of influence!

The next chapters deal with some core elements of horizontal leadership.

6.3.1 Four core leadership qualities

It is helpful for the horizontal leader to develop the above-mentioned four core leadership qualities for himself, and to enable others in the organisation to also train and make use of them:

- **Managing and Steering** physical and financial resources in processes; enabling others to manage and steer those in relative autonomy;
- **Coaching and Mentoring** others to support them doing their work, to support development of themselves and their individual skills for excellent performance and behaviour in processes;
- **Inspiring** individuals and teams by being able to explain the purpose of the organisation on every level, be it a small little step in a process, or be it the bigger picture; being able to give sense and meaning to it all;

- **Integrating and Intervening:** Integrating the context, sensing, asking the right questions, and coming to a good judgement about a situation; then when necessary, intervene for adjustments; understanding people's actions, lead in difficult meetings, integrate a broad range of skills and diverse behaviours and cultures; decide about new members to a team, together with the existing team members; decide if a team member has to leave, after a defined process of trying to integrate such team member; assign decision-making competences to teams and individuals.

Furthermore, horizontal leaders need the skill to design smart strategies, to create, together with their teams, the rules of behaviour which form the culture of working together. And finally, they need to be able to create, together with their teams, a shared purpose, a meaningful goal to which all members of the organisation like to relate to. Not everyone needs to be able to perform all of this; but the teams all-together should represent a full skill-set.

6.3.2 Seven beacons

As horizontal leaders we may consider for any organisation, whether a business, NGO, or university, or school, or hospital, or any other organisation, seven beacons. They can be taken like anchor points, like guiding signs, for analysing and improving the organisation. They can be used to analyse in which areas the organisation is strong and in which it is weak, and then focus on strengthening the weak areas, while not forgetting about the strong areas.

These seven beacons are, starting from the top: **1. Why**, **2. How**, **3. What**, **4. Who**, **5. Organisation**, **6. Processes**, **7. Resources (physical and financial)**. They are described in detail in the book "The Beacons Handbook for Taking Initiatives and Leading Change Projects. Concepts – Exercises – Tools", by Adriaan Bekman (free for download on www.het-imo.net/publications). I will describe them shortly here:

1. **Why:** The Why is about: why do we exist and whom are we serving? This is more than the traditional vision and mission. It includes the client's needs, the context in which we operate. It is outside-in and inside-out. What is the client expecting from us, and why is that so? Why do we want to serve the client with what we do? Without the Why, or the purpose, the organisation is aimless, struggling with conflicts, having lost power and energy for its true purpose. As mentioned, it is important that the Why is alive on all levels of the organisation. This includes telling stories and being able to break-down the more general mission into concrete small little actions. It includes being able to explain the Why on the example of every action within the organisation. To achieve that the discussion about the Why needs to be kept alive throughout the year in regular encounters and dialogues.

2. **How:** The How is about habits, behaviours, steering convictions, mind-sets, belief systems. All these determine the culture and the processes, rhythms and routines, of the organisation. Most of the organisations I see have not yet developed a good culture. Recent literature, like "The Culture Code" by Daniel Coyle, or

The Way of the Seal by Mark Divine, or Dare to Lead by Brené Brown represent a new set of books and knowledge about the culture of working together. One question can be: am I getting energy by working in this organisation, or is the behaviour of some people in my team dragging my energy, because there is – for instance – constant blaming and complaining about others? Another question could be: what is the deeper mind-set, or steering conviction behind a certain behaviour? If I want to change that behaviour, I need to change the mind-set, or steering principle, behind that behaviour.

3. **What:** The What is about strategy, the business plan, the annual budget, the key performance indicators. Many organisations I see are quite good at it. It is helpful – I find – to study, for instance, how companies like Microsoft, Amazon, or Berkshire Hathaway, develop and execute their strategies. One can really learn a lot by regularly reading their annual reports, all available for free on the internet.

4. The **Who** is about the initiative takers, the decision makers, the ones who take responsibility (on all levels), and their networks within the organisation.

5. The **Organisation** is about the responsibility, role, accountability, and decision-making authority of people in the organisation. It needs to be clear what kind of decisions can be made on which level and in which part of the client process. Horizontal organisations bring down decision-making to those places within the organisation which are nearest to the client, who

understand the client's needs best. They need to be enabled to make client-relevant decisions fast enough. A high level of transparency also financially is necessary, to create a delegated, efficient, and horizontal organisation.

6. **Process** is about all the processes within the organisation. It relates to phases, rhythms, time spans, repetitions, routines, beginnings, endings, deliveries, just-in-time, lean, well-prepared meetings, short meetings, effective meetings, good care for the actions listed in the protocol, enough time for reflection and recreation, and many other related issues. How to run a good meeting is a typical question on this level.

7. **Physical and Financial Resources** are about the resources and finances which are necessary to carry out the mission and strategy. It is about the level of investments, the office space, the building, the various warehouses, the quality of the office space for teams to work effectively and feel well, enough light, enough cash at hand, the level of debt, and so on.

The first three beacons are more theoretical, and the beacons five to seven are practical. Beacon four, the initiative takers, the people in the organisation, connect the beacons one to three with five to seven, and their interdependencies.

The seven beacons and their related leadership quality can be summarised as follows:

Beacon	Description	Leadership quality
Why	the mission, purpose, vision, and identity of the organisation	give sense and meaning
How	culture and behaviour, the way we work together, how we treat each other	live it, Be it
What	strategy, Key Performance Indicators	design and inspire
Who	initiative takers on all levels, knowing what the clients need	intervene, integrate
Organisation	who does what, responsibilities, roles, accountabilities	inspire
Process	effective, lean processes, carried out with good behaviour	coach and mentor
Resources	physical and financial means and resources	manage and steer

Table 4: Seven beacons

These seven beacons can be used in various ways:

- To analyse where the organisation stands in its development on each of these levels and use this analysis for improvements;
- To help everyone understand all levels and how they are interconnected;
- They can be a great way of motivating everyone if the leadership (on all levels) is able to explain and create full transparency on all levels; especially also, as mentioned earlier, to create financial transparency for the teams.

There are different ways to deal with the seven beacons. Their qualities can be found also in the qualities of the seven planets (Saturn, Jupiter, Mars, Sun, Venus, Mercury, Moon). Others, and I myself, do constant research in order to better understand these qualities, learn to better see them working in practical life, and research different ways to apply them for organisation change.

For the reader to see how colleagues in the field do their research and how these seven beacons can be used in different ways, I would like to present here one other way as developed by my colleague Hilmar Dahlem.

6.3.3 From question to process

From question to process is another way of dealing with the seven beacons:

1. It starts with **the question**. The question needs to be formulated and is the driving force behind the next steps. There is a reason for the question, a history has led to it, stories are related to it. All those need to be taken into account and be part of the question.
2. Then we take **the goal** into your focus. What do we want to achieve? What are concrete results and what are the criteria to measure success? What do we not want?
3. **Who is responsible?** Clarify roles, accountabilities, process owners, supporting experts, target groups, clients? Define tasks, but not all detail. Leave room for constant adjustment in view of the goal.
4. **How are you going to do it?** What are the steering principles which are guiding us? What kind of mindsets should drive our behaviour? What are the principles we want to use while leading the process?
5. **Time, process, and rhythms.** When do we start, when do we want to finish? Which are the phases and

steps during the process? Are there sub-processes necessary? Plan for regular and rhythmical meeting and communication cycles. What is the first step and what are next steps? Don't try to define everything to the maximum upfront. Lean and adjust on the way. Always work with the concept of the next step.

6. **What kind of resources do we need?** Think of money, rooms, tools, time, people, skills, and the like. Where do we expect resistance to achieving the goal, or resistance to change? Which kind of support do we need from responsible people in the organisation?

7. **Purpose. The Why.** Why do we need this project or change? Why is it important for the overall organisation to achieve this goal? What is the deeper meaning of it to which we can all relate our own individual purpose? If individual purpose and organisation purpose match the motivation increases.

This concept from question to process is a more practical way to deal with the seven beacons. It can be used for change projects within any organisation, or for individual development goals.

6.3.4 Focus on process

One of the things I do with my clients is to focus on process. I would invite all people involved in a key process around a long table. On the table there is one long paper. I would start by asking questions like: the client calls. What happens? One person would say: I take the call and enter the request into our database. I would ask: what happens next? The person says: I type the data also into another database. I interrupt and ask: really, another database? But that is double work! The person says: Yes, we know, but we have not found a better solution yet. Then we discuss, together with the "bosses" until we find the solution. We write everything on the long paper, the process itself, the event, the double typing, and the better solution. And we agree to a solution and who does what to implement the solution, and until when. Then we continue. I ask questions, they answer. Always very concrete and action oriented. As near as possible to the real process and how it happens. No big explanations. Just describe what happens.

This may sound simple. But each and every time I do this my clients are astonished how many things are not clear, which seemed to be clear to everyone. It is important that the "bosses" are at the table also. Because often they are the reason for processes which are not functioning well. Bosses, or leaders, or the founders, may believe they are clear to their employees, but often employees don't know what to do and how. By looking in such a simple way at processes this communication gap can be bridged. Things can be clarified sometimes in half a day.

Of course, there are many more complex processes. This then needs a different, more diligent process. In the IMO masterclasses participants learn how to look at such more complex processes in a more detailed way. They learn certain tools and methods how to do this. It is called IMO Lean, and Christian Lucke is specialised to teach this methodology in classes and work with it in client situations. Many of his clients are from industry and the corporate business world.

Another way to work with processes is to let the client give an example from his or her work, where a process does not work well. The client describes the example in all details. Often the facilitator has to ask concrete questions like: what colour was the shirt of the person you talked to? In which kind of room were you sitting? Were you sitting opposite to your colleague, or at corners, or next to him? Describe the process in all detail and action oriented. Don't explain ... and so on. The facilitator needs to support that clients do not explain all the knowledge behind such a process, but to stay with the facts and how they move in that concrete process.

Others in the room listen to the steering principles, the mind-sets behind this. After the client has described the process, the other persons in the room describe what they see as steering conviction, or the principles behind this. Examples might be: We want to pay our employees well; I am shy of speaking directly about the problematic issues at hand; we do not greet each other during the day; those who stay longest in the office do the best work; we discuss the easy issues first and the difficult issues last; we meet on Friday afternoon for our weekly meeting. The facilitator takes all notes on a flipchart so everyone can see it.

Then, all together, we write on a new flipchart what we want to change. It might look like this: For our weekly meeting we want to be fresh, and not tired, so we meet on Monday morning; we discuss the difficult issues first, we trust that some of the easy issues will solve themselves, ... and so on.

6.3.5 Process ownership

In horizontal leadership we work with the concept of process ownership. That is different from project management in the sense that it is less about an exact definition of the whole project, but more about getting things done in small incremental steps, learning on the way. A typical project manager defines the process as complete and in as much detail as possible upfront, then designs a project team, and in the course of the project supports and controls progress and time management.

A process owner would start with a rough image of the goal and purpose of the task at hand, builds a team if necessary, assigns certain tasks and roles, which are also not too specific in their description, and then moves ahead fast, learning on the way, adjusting immediately if necessary, communicating very immediately to everyone involved. On the way the goal can become more specific. The results are immediate, but in small next steps. It is highly motivating. A process owner can be anyone in the organisation, independent from the hierarchical position. A process can start somewhere, and end at another place when the task is done. It can be for smaller tasks, like organising for coffee and some light food for a meeting, or bigger tasks like organising classes, part tasks in bigger projects, and many other situations.

The concept of process ownership is able to relieve managers and employees from many tasks and meetings related to project management. Many companies, especially for instance in the automotive industry, have an overkill of projects to manage, including too many and too long meetings. For many of those tasks a process owner could be assigned to care for the performance of the task. Talking about process also means to learn to "go with the flow", to learn to see how things evolve in movement and the need to constant careful attention for potential adjustments. This needs a different way of looking at things. It includes the dimension of time and flow into the dimension of space. We are trained to look at things in space, but not so much yet to look at things in movement. If we do this, we may notice that many things on the way solve themselves and that it is not necessary to control everything, which is the tendency with project management. The task would be to find out for which tasks project management is still the right concept, and which tasks can be done in the form of process ownership.

I will give a simple example of how one could use the concept of process owner in preparing and running a meeting. 1. The team agrees to one of them to be process owner (PO) for a certain task including some decision-making rights. 2. The team agrees that in case the team does not find an agreement to a certain decision that then the PO may decide in the best interest of the goal at hand and the overall goal of the company. The team agrees to accept that decision. 3. The PO prepares a rough draft of the process, provides it to the team and leads a dialogue with the team. The PO cares for a good process of such dialogue, mainly he takes care that people listen to each other and that everyone in the room speaks roughly the same amount of time. 4. The PO formulates a decision which suits everyone, which everyone can agree to and be motivated to act on. If that is the case all together come to a decision and start acting on it. 5. If an agreement cannot be found, if there are two opposing opinions in the room, and if the PO is not able to find a bridge between those two opposing approaches, then he asks the team for allowing him to make the final decision. The team then accepts that decision and acts accordingly.

This approach has elements of "I disagree, but I commit". It is something we need to learn that not always my own way will be the right way but that there are many different ways to achieve a goal. This approach, if prepared and led well by the PO is very much time effective and motivating.

6.3.6 Transformative exercises

Horizontal leadership trainings go very deep with regard to the three elements of process, dialogue, and biography. This going deep is done with the help of so-called exercises. Such exercises are small group settings which can be used in workshop and in real work situations. They form an important part of horizontal leadership, of creating harmony in the soul, of letting the "I" of the other appear. Without such exercises, the rest would be only theory. Through these exercises, theory can be immediately experienced by the participants.

In workshops and master classes around the world, it can be experienced again and again that these exercises are of transformative quality. Participants tell each other about their challenges, questions, and successes. They listen deeply and generatively. This happens in a very intimate atmosphere, and with the help of a structured process in which people can feel psychologically safe. Participants speak about their real issues. It is not a role play. It is always the authentic "I" in the soul which shows in these exercises. That makes it sometimes very challenging for the participants. The effect, however, of such exercises is transformative in the sense that people change through doing them. Feedback is given in a free and respectful form. Trust is being created, a better understanding of each other appears, enthusiasm and laughter comes after the exercise and refreshes everyone involved.

The workshop leader has to introduce the exercise very carefully and then care for that the rules are being kept. For instance, no smartphones may be used during such exercises. IMO has developed seven basic exercises, which are described in detail in the book Inside the Change by Adriaan Bekman.[47] There are many variations of these, and other exercises, being used by IMO consultants.

The seven basic exercises are:

---

47 Bekman, Adriaan: "Inside the Change", free for download at www.het-imo.net

- Find and adjust the guiding image;
- Questioning the question;
- Clarify the vision;
- Improve work processes;
- Find and adjust the steering principle;
- Setting up the inner voices and team;
- Design scenarios for the future.

The key for successful exercises is a clear process, and the right question asked. It is one of the main tasks of the facilitator, to develop those questions which meet the questions of the people involved.

The exercise "questioning the question" is especially interesting as an example of how transformation takes place during such an exercise. The process design is like this, in groups of three: A takes one minute to think about her or his question and writes it down. Then she speaks about it for three minutes. B is asking clarifying questions. C is only listening and observing. Then A will take one minute, rethink her question, and again write it down. After one minute, A speaks again for three minutes about her question. B asks clarifying questions. Then something nice happens: B tells A about something of personal interest with enthusiasm, like a hobby, or a nice event which happened recently, and which made B enthusiastic. It is important that B tells something which is full of positive energy so that B's eyes are shining and his voice is strong. It has nothing to do with A's question. This takes five minutes. Then A takes again one minute and reflects about how she will formulate the question now. Writing it down is helpful. And after one minute, A reads the final version of her question and describes her next step. As a final step A, B and C have a free dialogue about what was talked about. This last step is relieving the tension and anything which comes into mind can be shared. It is also a wonderful way of giving some feedback or tip. Then the next in the group takes the role of A so that at the end of the exercise everyone in the group of three has been in the role of A. This may take a bit more than an hour. As facilitator I usually listen carefully to the sound of the voices in the room. This helps me to notice how the dialogues are going. It is joyful to see the smiling faces when B tells his or her story and to listen to the raising sound and laughter in the room!

It is very interesting to see how the question changes, develops, evolves, through this exercise. Normally participants believe that they know their questions. Some even say they do not have a question. They claim to be clear in their vision and lives. It may happen then that the other participants notice that this person is not clear at all. The described exercise can be very helpful for clarifying my own question. But this only works well if the others in the group are listening carefully and deeply.

6.3.7 Deep listening

During the above mentioned TheoryU Masterclass I learned about deep listening. Scharmer explained that there are four levels of listening: downloading, listen to information, listen to emotion, listen to will and intention.

The information relates to thinking. The emotion relates to feeling. The intention relates to the will. Downloading is a form of not really listening to the information, but "knowing" already what comes. When somebody starts speaking and I already know what he or she is going to say – Scharmer calls this downloading.

The deepest way of listening is when I listen generatively. To listen generatively relates to the level of the will, or the intention. When I listen generatively, the attention and presence of me, the listener, is determining what the speaker is able to say. The listener literally helps the speaker to "generate" his words and ideas. Deep, or generative listening, creates trust, because people will open up and speak about their personal and professional challenges. Sharing those challenges is a strong force for building, or re-building, trust amongst team members.

In deep listening, the quality of listening is more important than what the speaker has prepared to say. Normally in business, we are busy with finding the next moment when we are speaking up again, loud enough, with some thoughts and ideas. In generative listening, this activity is turned towards the listener. Her or his attention and presence while listening, not talking, determine what is being said by the other person. Meetings become more meaningful, more effective and shorter with the help of deep listening. The quality of listening is one element of the culture of the organisation. Deep listening and holding the space with empathy has a healing effect for the challenges and pains of the other person.

6.3.8 High-performance teams

How I behave, how my intervention affects others, depends on my inner state of being, as mentioned above. This inner state of being is the determining factor. If I am in a harmonious and peaceful inner state of being, I am also able to act more effectively in teams and processes. Inner states of being can change from one moment to the next. Then I reveal my weaknesses and shadows. It needs training to regain an emotionally harmonious state, and to keep it in difficult and stress situations.

Here are some characteristics about how to build a high-performing culture, how high-performance-teams interact with each other and in processes, inspired by Daniel Coyle's "The Culture Code":

Build safety:
- Team members must feel safe when speaking about their challenges; they should have a lot of short, energetic exchanges about small successes and failures; they care that everyone talks to everyone; they ask a lot of questions; they intensively and actively listen; they have a lot of humour and laughter; they perform many small, attentive courtesies like thank-you, opening doors, etc.; they treat every person as unique and valued; the team leader signals that the relationship will continue;
- Everyone in the group talks and listens in roughly equal amounts of time, keeping contributions short;
- Team-members maintain a high level of eye contact; their conversations and gestures are energetic; they communicate directly with each other;
- Feedback is given all the time, especially in daily after-action reviews; everyone gives feedback to everyone, including the team leader;
- Group performance depends on behaviour that communicates one powerful overarching idea: we are safe and connected! We share a future!

Share Vulnerability
- Success does not depend so much on individual skills but on the ability to combine those skills into a greater purpose;
- As a leader send a really clear signal that you have weaknesses and that you could use help; if that behaviour becomes a model for others, then you can set

aside the insecurities and share your challenges and by that increase the trust in each other;
- Then people relax and connect, and are able to bring their best performance;
- In a good team, a teammate may falter; others sense it and respond by taking on more pain for the sake of the group; balance is regained;
- This requires that I as a teammate sense my action while constantly sensing the action of the others, and their state of feeling and being; by sensing and reaction to any change very fast, the team is able to decide and act in a very agile way;
- Give immediate feedback; feedback is never meant to be personal; feedback is never taken personally; we joke and laugh a lot; we listen well; regularly we do an after-action-review and give rigorous feedback; we make feedback smaller, more targeted, less personal, less judgemental, impactful, always maintaining the sense of safety and belonging;
- We avoid the traditional performance review; instead, we focus on development and strength, providing support and opportunities for growth.
- Create behaviour rules for your team, like: we ask for help anytime when we need it; we do not blame each other; when a teammate falters, we help; we do small steps in view of the big goal; we learn always and incrementally; we share our learning; endlessly repeat and remodel such behaviour; this creates a larger conceptual framework that connects with the group's identity and expresses the core purpose; match this set of rules and priorities with training, staff meetings, and all communications.

Create a Shared Purpose
- Successful teams relentlessly tell and retell their story about the shared and common purpose;
- Use a single story to orient the motivation towards the meaningful future; this should work like a magnetic field, giving orientation where to go, like: this is why we work, here is where you should put your energy;
- High-purpose environments are filled with small, vivid signals designed to create a link between the present moment and a future ideal: we are currently here, and this is where we want to go;
- The goal must be realistic; the obstacles and challenges must be clear;
- The challenge of building purpose is to translate abstract ideas (values, mission, The Why) into concrete terms. One way successful groups do this is by spotlighting a single task and using it to define their identity, set the bar for their expectations, and link it in simple words with the overall goals;
- Build purpose around spotlighting a small, effortful behaviour.

And finally:
- Hire people smarter than you;
- Fail early, get better every time;
- Listen well to everyone's ideas;
- Face the problems;

- It is more important to invest in good people than in good ideas, or even in certain cases in skill and experience;
- Take a lot of time and attention to attend to team members feeling safe, to their composition and dynamics;
- Take a great effort to support failing and misbehaving team members in their development to the better; if the intended development – after due time – does not take place – then say goodbye; the process until saying goodbye should be very transparent upfront, everyone should know it;
- Create a positive departure culture for those who leave the team and organisation;
- Define, reinforce, and relentlessly protect the team's creative autonomy;
- Make it safe to fail and to give immediate feedback;
- Celebrate hugely when the group takes initiative;
- Create fun and a little weirdness, for the purpose of good humour and a joking atmosphere.

I have described new ways of working together in a horizontal way, based on the image of the threefold human being. In this way I am not only using my brain to think and my muscles to execute, but also my heart and feelings to listen, sense, see, and execute with empathy.

6.3.9 Organisationdevelopment

How does organisationdevelopment happen? There are many different ways to do this. There are more than 50 years of worldwide experience with change projects. There is a vast amount of literature, research, and science, available about it. However, many change projects are not successful. I recently read that a number of 50% of all change projects fail. In my experience change projects fail when the necessary change in the people is not being addressed properly, when not all people are committed to the change, when they are not properly involved, and when expectations are too short term.

This is why I put people first. First, I have to learn to connect to myself and become more aware of how I can bring my inner world in a better relationship with the outer world around me. I need enough self-love in order to be able to empathise with others. When I am in good contact with myself, when I am self-confident, I can look at the organisation and necessary changes there. For this I can use either the seven areas of attention and analyse which areas need improvement, or I use the concept 'From question to process', or I use one of the many other existing tools in the literature and organisationdevelopment practice. It is essential that my inner purpose and motivation can relate and ideally unite with the purpose of the organisation. As facilitator I am facilitating such processes. It must be clear for the client that change processes take a long time. People are able and willing to change. But often it is not easy, and it takes years. To be realistic I suggest to my clients that any real change process will take at least 2 – 3 years. But on the way already many smaller and bigger changes can be affected.

6.4 The organisation as a living being

The organisation is a living being, made up of human beings, their souls, their strengths and weaknesses, their habits and behaviours, their biographies. The dimension of the biography also takes into account the respective age of the people in the organisation. It is a difference whether someone is 35, or 40, and naturally ambitious and competitive in the best way, or if someone is 55 or 60 and is not so busy anymore with her or his own career development and is therefore more able to care for others.

Adriaan Bekman writes in his book "The Human Creation": "The human soul is fully reflected in the organisations that man has created and is creating. All that a human soul is capable of appears in an organisation. Organisations require maintenance, care, change, and renewal. They have no other sense and meaning than the sense and meaning people themselves give them." This giving meaning to the organisation is a task of all of us. To this task we can wake up and take responsibility. As humans we are challenged to develop ourselves, together with others, in organisations, at our workplace. Everyone is part of the leadership that takes place as a process in this. It offers us the opportunity to appear as an authentic individuality to other people. By asking the right question, the other person is able show her or his authentic self. The right question supports that I become fully awake in the presence of the moment. In dialogue with the other person I will be able to find some answers and make the next step in my development.

This way of self-development together with others is relatively new and is the way of learning I am attempting to describe in this book. It starts with the question and leads to people meeting each other and getting into a meaningful dialogue, including their biographies, their successes, and challenges, their pains and sufferings, their light, and shadows. In a good process, together, with the help of the other, we are able to understand our situations better, we are able to give it meaning and purpose. Together we are better able to reach out to our higher Self, our "I", and by that to the spiritual with ideas and concepts, taking into account intuitions and subtle premonitions of future events. Together we are able to grasp those ideas in a good conversation and take note of it, write it down, or remember it. Together then we are able to give meaning to the organisations in which we live and work, at home and at the workplace, by doing the next step.

This way of learning complements the other way of learning, which is through retreat, concentration, and meditation. Both ways of learning are necessary. Many people today are not so easily able to do self-reflection and meditation anymore. They find it hard to concentrate long enough to get substantial results. Therefore, the way of learning and doing things together becomes more important nowadays. Many people find their destiny through a good dialogue, including deep listening. The dialogue then becomes the room to better understand my own life's mission and karma.

7.
Fully human

I have started this book by looking at AI and the challenge it presents to us as human beings. This challenge can be put into the following question: what does it mean to be fully human and how are we able to keep control over our own human values in a world full of machines?

To find some answers to this question I have looked at the human being in a threefold way, attempting to summarise some of the more recent scientific findings about the brain, the heart, and how movement takes place. The result of this research reveals that the human being and its functioning is not only based on the brain and its activity. The brain being part of the nerve-and-senses system is mainly there to support sensing, coordinating, and cognition. It allows us to think, to cognise, to sense, to reflect, to make sense of the world around us. It functions as a mirror to our consciousness and by this we can be conscious human beings.

However, the brain cannot feel. And it is not able to carry out complex movements of the body on its own. It is our higher Self, our "I" which is the active factor in thinking, feeling, and willing. The "I" shows itself as a power within the mind, as warmth and interest, as enthusiasm, as a force which is able to use thinking, feeling, and willing, to decide freely, to think, feel, and act consciously. It uses those three soul entities to realise its goals, its biography. And thinking, feeling, and willing each have their "own" physiological basis: the thinking in the nerves-and-senses system, feeling in the heart-rhythm system, and willing in the metabolic-limbs system. Regarding the heart and rhythmic system, I described some of the findings which point to the key role of the heart and lung, and their working together in breathing and heart-rhythm, their key role in the context of mind, soul, and body. I need my heart to come to a good judgement.

When I point to myself, I do not point to my head or brain; I point to my heart. With the help of my heart I can feel what is right or wrong, I can feel the thoughts being cold or warm. Every one of my feelings also affects my breathing rhythm. With the help of breathing techniques, I am able to slow down and calm exited feelings. For so many things in life I first feel it and only later I am able to express it, put it into context, think about it. I am able to train my awareness for feelings and emotions. I can work with my emotions and it is possible over time to purify them and to create more harmony in the soul. This enables the soul to better reach into the realm of inspiration, ideals, and enthusiasm. This harmony then enables me to become a better team player, for more ego-free decision-making.

The most difficult question is the question of who moves, or of how movement takes place. I attempted to put some non-conclusive thoughts together which hopefully give the reader a direction for further reflection. I pointed to the "I" being active inside and outside at the same time. Hans Jürgen Scheurle[48] points to the brain as being an organ of resonance in constant communication with the inside and the outside.

My conclusion about the human being is that the human "I"

---

48   Scheurle, Hans Jürgen: "Das Gehirn ist nicht einsam. Resonanzen zwischen Gehirn, Leib und Umwelt", Stuttgart 2017

is a spiritual, non-local entity, which lives in the heart, the true centre of the human being. I can feel and act from my heart. I am able to develop my heart into a sensing organ. And by making good judgements, I use my heart as an organ of conscience and cognition. From my heart, I am able to notice and feel my thoughts coming to me in the form of ideas, concepts, and opinions. It is the spiritual "I", the individuality itself, it is me, who does all. From my heart I realise my ideals in the material world.

This then can be applied to our modern organisation life. I asked the question: how do I find the other? How do we build teams and communities, based on common ideals? For this we need leadership based on self-development. This has led me to put together some of the basic concepts of creating harmony in the soul in order to better be able to work together with others in horizontal and vertical leadership situations and organisations.

I wanted to show some aspects of being fully human in a world full of machines. AI can be a call for us to look at ourselves more closely and to find and realise the huge potential of human skills, creativity, ideas, and ideals, of being fully human.

Stuttgart, Autumn 2019

8.
Acknowledgements

I deeply thank all those who helped me in writing this book:

My friends from the heart circle. We are working on the many questions related to the heart, the human being, and its relation to the cosmos since 2007. This work has and still is hugely inspiring for my life and work.

Prof. Dr Adriaan Bekman, the founder of IMO, who encouraged me several times to start writing, and from whom are many of the concepts in this book.

The group of now more than 50 consultants from 9 countries of IMO Institute for Man and Organisation Development.

The small working group we have is related to artificial intelligence and its challenges and benefits.

My friends from whom I learned during the last 55 years. There are many, and I thank you.

All my work relationships, some not always easy, that helped me to get grounded and develop a solid life and work experience, and a deep understanding of the human being, including its shadows and light.

My wife and my family, who continue to encourage and support me.

Dr. med. Michaela Gloeckler, who invited me in 2015 to start giving courses in Asia, which opened a whole new field of activity and learning for me, getting to know many new friends and participants, many of whom indirectly contributed to this book.

Out of this activity we were able to start IMO China in March 2019 in Beijing.

Tertta Paananen, Timothy Apps, Susanne and Torodd Lien, and a few other friends, who took the effort to read the book carefully and who gave me many good tips for improvement.

Luis Espiga who supported my writing in many deep dialogues with his wisdom and life experience, and who wrote the preface to this book.

And finally M. S. and M. S., who took the role as editor, taking a big effort by digging deep into each sentence and into the thought-flow of the chapters. This really gave the book the final push and shape. Thank you!

9.
Biographical note

I am an executive coach and I work with my clients and partners on their leadership- and organisationdevelopment questions. I do this worldwide, with a focus on Europe and Asia. In 2019 I was part of starting IMO China.

Before 2014, I was working for more than 20 years in Finance and Banking in various operational and leadership positions. I started my career working for Hewlett Packard, then Deutsche Bank, and since 1999 for Triodos Bank, Netherlands, first as fund manager, then as managing director. As fund manager I started a new private equity fund for investments into renewable energy and organic food, and as managing director I was a co-founder of the German branch of the bank. During these years I was able to serve in many different positions, from employee, to partner/owner, to manager and leader, to managing director, in a hierarchy, and to many different supervisory board positions in small and medium-sized organisations. This book is based on those practical experiences.

I currently hold several advisory and supervisory board positions, amongst them are Klinik Arlesheim (CH), Aarstiderne (DK), Kulturland eG (DE), Purpose Foundation and Venture Fund (DE), ELIANT (BE), Triforminstitute (SE).

Contact information:

alexschwedeler@gmx.net
alexanderschwedeler.de
schwedeler@het-imo.net
[het-imo.net](het-imo.net)

10.
The Galileo Report

Galileo Commission Report. Summary of Argument

1. No human intellectual activity, including science, can escape the fact that it has to make assumptions that cannot be proven using its own methodology (absolute presuppositions).

2. The prevalent underlying assumptions, or world model, of the majority of modern scientists are narrowly naturalist in metaphysics, materialist in ontology, and reductionist-empiricist in methodology.

3. This results in the belief that consciousness is nothing but a consequence of complex arrangement of matter, or an emergent phenomenon of brain activity.

4. This belief is neither proven, nor warranted.

5. In fact, there are well documented empirical phenomena that contradict this belief. Among them are

   a. Veridical reports of near-death experiences (NDEs) with complex intuitions, perceptions, cognitions, and emotions during well-documented absence of brain activity.

   b. Veridical reports of non- ocal perception that were confirmed independently during such near-death states of absent brain activity.

   c. The large database of parapsychology and anomalous cognition research shows in a series of meta-analyses that such non-local perceptions are indeed possible.

   d. The large database of children who remember previous lives, some of whom have corresponding deformities.

6. An increasing number of open-minded scientists are already researching these frontier areas using existing scientific methods and are reaching empirically grounded conclusions that challenge the mainstream majority view.

7. They therefore argue that we need a model of consciousness that is non-reductive and allows consciousness its own ontological status.

8. A minimum-consensus model is a dual aspect or complementarity model, in which matter and mind, consciousness and its physical substrate, are two aspects of reality that are irreducible and simultaneously occurring perspectives of an underlying reality to which we otherwise have no direct access.

9. If that is granted, we can immediately see that consciousness can have its own direct access to reality, not only through sense perception, as in classical empiricism, but also through inner perception or radical introspection.

10. As a result, there may be a different and valid access route to reality, through consciousness, in addition to the classical one science is offering.

11. This might include direct access, under certain conditions, to deeper structures of reality, which may provide important insights into ethics, meaning, and values.

12. Indeed, insights from NDEs and other transformative experiences suggest that we are all embedded within a larger field of consciousness, with profound implications for ethics in an interconnected world.

13. Integrating an enlarged view of consciousness into science will also yield a new methodology that will have to be developed: the methodology of radical introspection or inner experience in which matter and mind, consciousness and its physical

substrate, are two aspects of reality that are irreducible and simultaneously occurring perspectives of an underlying reality to which we otherwise have no direct access.

14. In view of the widespread perception that a narrow materialist worldview is often uncritically passed on to young scientists by mainstream authorities as an adequate explanation of reality and as a pre-conditon for a successful scientific career, we call for an open exploration of this topic and we encourage the scientific community to become more critically self- reflective of the absolute presuppositions on which their activities are based and to consider expanding their scope.

The Galileo Commission

It is for all these reasons that we have set up the Galileo Commission (www. galileocommission.org) as a project of the Scientific and Medical Network (www. scimednet.org). The Commission is represented by a distinguished group of scientific advisers listed in Appendix B and is co-ordinated by a small committee. The Network (see Appendix A) has been working at the interface between science, spirituality, and consciousness since the 1970s, and has an open membership dedicated to exploring and expanding our horizons in these fields. Our major annual conferences include Mystics and Scientists in April (www. mysticsandscientists.org) and Introduction to Philosophical Materialism with its associated concept of a purposeless universe and the inherent meaninglessness of life is correlated with economic materialism with its emphasis on consumerism and the exploitation of people and natural resources. This translates into the idea that consumption and economic growth are the route to happiness and well-being. Many leading thinkers such as Martin Seligman (Diener and Seligman, 2004) are now questioning this association between consumption and well-being, with a renewed Beyond the Brain Conference in November (www.beyondthebrain.org).

Literature

Arendt, Hannah: *Über das Urteilen*

Allen, David: *Getting Things Done: The Art of Stress-Free Productivity*

Augstein, Jakob: *Reclaim Autonomy. Selbstermächtigung in der digitalen Weltordnung*

Barrat, James: *Our Final Invention. Artificial Intelligence and the End of the Human Era*

Beauregard, Mario: *The Spiritual Brain. A Neuroscientist's Case for the Existence of the Soul.*

Bekman, Adriaan: *The Human Creation. A Philosophy of Organised Life.*

Bekman, Adriaan: *Inside the Change,*

Bekman, Adriaan: *The Horizontal Leadership Book* and all other books by him see www.het-imo.net.

Bekman, Adriaan: *Die Menschliche Schöpfung. Philosophie des organisierten Lebens. Über die Frage nach unserem Ursprung, nach unserer Seele und unserer Freiheit in Organisationen*

Bernstein, Gabrielle: *Judgement Detox. Release the Beliefs That Hold You Back from Living a Better Life*

Bernstein, Gabrielle: *The Universe Has Your Back. How to Feel Safe and Trust Your Life No Matter What*

Bossidi, Larry: *Execution. The Discipline of Getting Things Done*

Bostrom, Nick: *Superintelligenz. Szenarien einer kommenden Revolution*

Brown, Brené: *Daring Greatly. How the Courage to be Vulnerable Transforms the Way We Live, Love, Parent, and Lead*

Brown, Brené: *Dare To Lead. Brave Work. Tough Conversations. Whole Hearts*

Burchard, Brendon: *High Performance Habits. How Extraordinary People Become That Way*

Buffet, Warren: *Berkshire Hathaway. Letters to Shareholders 1965 – 2017.* All Shareholder Letters as part of the Annual Reports see www.berkshirehathaway.com, and Tap Dancing to Work (his biography)

Care, Nessa: *The Epigenetics Revolution. How Modern Biology is Rewriting our Understanding of Genetics, Disease and Inheritance*

Charam, Ram: *Boards That Lead. When to Take Charge, When to Partner, and When to Stay Out of the Way*

Children, Doc: *Heart Intelligence. Connecting with the Intuitive Guidance of the Heart*

Children, Doc: *The Heartmath Solution. The Institute of HeartMath's Revolutionary Program for Engaging the Power of the Heart's Intelligence*

Chopra, Deepak with Kafatos, Menas. *You Are the Universe. Discovering Your Cosmic Self and Why It Matters*

Clark, David: *The Tao of Charlie Munger. A Compilation of Quotes from Berkshire Hathaway's Vice Chairman on Life, Business, and the Pursuit of Wealth With Commentary by David Clark*

Covey, Stephen R.: *First Things First*

Covey, Stephen R.: *7 Habits Of Highly Effective People*

Cowan, Thomas: *Human Heart, Cosmic Heart. A Doctor s Quest to Understand, Treat, and Prevent Cardiovascular Disease*

Coyle, Daniel: *The Culture Code. The Secrets of Highly Successful Groups*

Cunningham, Lawrence: *Berkshire Beyond Buffett. The Enduring Value of Values*

Dalio, Ray: *Principles. Life and Work*

Daugherty, Paul R.: *Human + Machine. Reimagining Work in the Age of AI*

Denning, Stephen: *The Age of Agile. How Smart Companies Are Transforming the Way Work Gets Done*

Divine, Mark: *The Way of the SEAL. Think Like An Elite Warrior to Lead and Succeed*

Edelhäuser, Friedrich: *Beim Wahrnehmen und Bewegen lebt das Ich in der Welt. Zur Funktion des menschlichen Nervensystems,* Vortrag, Stuttgart 2011

Edmondson, Amy C.: *Extreme Teaming. Lessons in Complex, Cross-Sector Leadership*

Elrod, Hal: *The Miracle Morning. The Not-So-Obvious Secret Guaranteed to Transform Your Life*

Elworthy, Scilla: *Pioneering the Possible. Awakened Leadership for a World That Works*

Enright, Robert: *8 Keys to Forgiveness*

Fingerhut et al. (Ed.): *Philosophie der Verkörperung*

Fuchs, Thomas: *Das Gehirn – ein Beziehungsorgan. Eine phänomenologisch-ökologische Konzeption*

Furst, Branko: *The Heart and Circulation. An Integrative Model*

Gardner, Howard: *Five Minds for the Future*

Gartland, Tom: *Lead with Heart. Transform Your Business Through Personal Connection*

Gilbert, Paul: *The Compassionate Mind*

Graf, Richard: *Die neue Entscheidungskultur. Mit gemeinsam getragenen Entscheidungen zum Erfolg*

Gostick, Adrian and Elton, Chester: *The Best Team Wins. The New Science of High Performance*

Amit Goswami, PhD: *The Everything Answer Book. How Quantum Science explains Love, Death and the Meaning of Life*

Heusser, Peter: *Anthroposophy and Science. An Introduction*

Häusling, André, Römer, Esther and Zeppenfeld, Nina: *Praxisbuch Agilität*

Häusling, André: *Agile Organisationen. Transformationen erfolgreich gestalten – Beispiele agiler Pioniere*

Hawking, Stephen, *Autonomous Weapons. An Open Letter from AI & Robotics Researchers.* Future of life Institute (28. 7. 2015).

Hawkins, David R: *Power vs. Force*

Hofstetter, Yvonne: *Sie wissen alles. Wie intelligente Maschinen in unser Leben eindringen und warum wir für unsere Freiheit kämpfen müssen*

Hoystad, Ole Martin: *Kulturgeschichte des Herzens. Von der Antike bis zur Gegenwart*

Judith, Anodea, Goodman, Lion: *Creating on Purpose. The Spiritual Technology of Manifesting Through the Chakras*

Judith, Anodea: *The Global Heart Awakens. Humanity's Rite of Passage from the Love of Power to the Power of Love*

Judith, Anodea: *Chakras Made Easy. Seven Keys to Awakening and Healing the Energy Body*

Kahane, Adam: *Collaborating with the Enemy. How to Work with People You Don't Agree with or Like or Trust*

Kethledge, Raymond M., Erwin, Michael S.: *Lead Yourself First. Inspiring Leadership Through Solitude*

Kurzweil, Ray, Rötzschke, Martin: *Menschheit 2.0: Die Singularität naht*

Lamb, Gary, Hearn, Sarah: *Steinerian Economics. A Compendium*

Lama, Dalai, Tutu, Desmond: *The Book of Joy*

Leaky, Maren: *Die 10 größten Führungsfehler und wie Sie sie vermeiden*

Lewis, Bill: *100 Mistakes of a Start Up CEO*

Mackey, John, Sisodia, Raj et al.: *Conscious Capitalism. Liberating the Heroic Spirit of Business*

Merkel, Miriam: *Mein Kopf gehört mir. Eine Reise durch die schöne Welt des Brainhacking*

Nadella, Satya, Shaw, Greg, Nichols, Jill Tracie: *Hit Refresh. The Quest to Rediscover Microsoft's Soul and Imagine a Better Future for Everyone*

Newport, Cal: *Deep Work. Rules for Focused Success in a Distracted World*

Anderson, Chris: *Ted Talks. The official TED guide to public speaking: Tips and tricks for giving unforgettable speeches and presentations*

Oesterreich, Bernd, Schröder, Claudia: *Das kollegial geführte Unternehmen. Ideen und Praktiken für die agile Organisation von morgen*

Ohlsberg, Karl: *Boy in the White Room*

Pinchbeck, Daniel: *How Soon is Now. From Personal Initiation to Global Transformation*

Pransky, Jillian: *Deep Listening. A Healing Practice to Calm Your Body, Clear Your Mind, and Open Your Heart*

Robertson, Brian J.: *The Revolutionary Management System that Abolishes Hierarchy*

Rohen, Johannes W.: *Die funktionale Struktur von Mensch und Gesellschaft: Elementare Funktionsprinzipien im menschlichen und sozialen Organismus*

Rohen, Johannes W.: *Eine funktionelle und spirituelle Anthropologie unter Einbeziehung der Menschenkunde Rudolf Steiners*

Rohen, Johannes W.: *Functional Morphology. The Dynamic Wholeness of the Human Organism*

Rohen, Johannes W.: *Functional Threefoldness in the Human Organism and Human Society*

Rohen, Johannes W.: *Die sozialen Probleme der modernen Gesellschaft. Anregungen zu einer zeitgemäßen Lösung*

Rothblatt, Martine: *Virtually Human. The Promise and the Peril of Digital Immortality*

Rosslenbroich, Bernd: *On the Origin of Autonomy. A New Look at the Major Transitions in Evolution*

Scharmer, Otto: *TheoryU. Leading from the Future as It Emerges*

Schein, Edgar H.: *Humble Consulting. How to Provide Real Help Faster*

Scheurle, Hans Jürgen: *Das Gehirn ist nicht einsam. Resonanzen zwischen Gehirn, Leib und Umwelt*

Schneier on Security Blog, see https://www.schneier.com

Schroeder, Alice: *The Snowball. Warren Buffet and the Business of Life*

Schultz, Howard: *Onward. How Starbucks Fought for Its Life Without Losing Its Soul*

Schwab, Klaus: *The Fourth Industrial Revolution*

Shimoff, Marci: *Love for No Reason. 7 Steps to Creating a Life of Unconditional Love*

Sinek, Simon: *Start With Why. How Great Leaders Inspire Everyone to Take Action*

Sinek, Simon: *Leaders Eat Last. Why Some Teams Pull Together and Others Don't*

Sprenger, Reinhard K.: *Radikal führen*

Sprenger, Reinhard K.: *Radikal digital. Weil der Mensch den Unterschied macht – 111 Führungsrezepte*

Sprenger, Reinhard K.: *Das Anständige Unternehmen. Was richtige Führung ausmacht – und was sie weglässt*

Steiner, Rudolf: *Knowledge of the Higher Worlds*

Steiner, Rudolf: *An Outline of Occult Science*

Steiner, Rudolf: The *Philosophy of Spiritual Activity*

Steiner, Rudolf: *Von Seelenrätseln*

Stone, Douglas, Heen, Sheila: *Thanks for the Feedback. The Science and Art of Receiving Feedback Well*

Suarez, Daniel: *Daemon, and other fiction books by him*

Trojanow, Ilija und Juli Zeh: *Angriff auf die Freiheit. Sicherheitswahn, Überwachungsstaat und der Abbau bürgerlicher Rechte*

Vitale, Joe, Len, Ihaleakala Hew: *Zero Limits. The Secret Hawaiian System for Wealth, Health, Peace, and More*

Vitale, Joe: *At Zero. The Final Secrets to "Zero Limits". The Quest for Miracles Through Ho'oponopono*

Warnke, Ulrich: *Quantenphilosophie und Spiritualität. Der Schlüssel zu den Geheimnissen des menschlichen Seins*

Wakeman, Cy: *No Ego. How Leaders Can Cut the Cost of Workplace Drama, End Entitlement, and Drive Big Results*

Watkins, Alan: *Coherence. The Secret Science of Brilliant Leadership*

Wiesing, Lambert (Ed.): *Philosophie der Wahrnehmung. Modelle und Reflexionen*

12. Further readings

https://dawnofhearts.org

https://eliant.eu/en/home/

http://fully-human.org

https://www.het-imo.net

https://www.heartmath.com

https://www.galileocommission.org

https://www.huffpost.com/entry/toward-a-postmaterialistic-science

https://www.interaliamag.org/articles/mario-beauregard/

https://www.scienceandnonduality.com

https://www.tsc2019-interlaken.ch